ADVANCE PRAISE FOR
UP: INFLUENCE POWER AND THE U PERSPECTIVE - THE ART OF GETTING WHAT YOU WANT

This book is an invaluable tool for any executive in any industry; it reveals an infallible strategy for success.

Charles Wardell, Managing Director, Korn Ferry International

The key to success in business is your ability to influence others. This book provides a unique approach that will help you get what you want in any situation.

Harold Bosworth, Chief Merchandising Officer, Talbots

Lee's U Perspective puts everything into perspective, reinforcing his approach to influencing throughout without the redundancy that makes so many books of this type virtually unreadable. A great read that delivers pearls of wisdom along the way.

Joan Verplanck, President, NJ Chamber of Commerce

If only everybody implemented the U Perspective how much more successful could they be! This simple, clear concept makes perfect sense for any interaction. Everyone should run out and buy a copy of *UP* immediately!

Julie Jansen, Author,*I Don't Know What I Want But I Know It's Not This*

This book is a must read for any woman who ever feels "Things would be great if they would only see it my way!" Lee offers practical, proven success strategies to help influence outcomes. Understanding how to use the U Perspective will assist anyone who wants to get things done through and with others.

Jean M. Otte, CEO Women Unlimited &
Author, *Changing the Corporate Landscape*

With what Miller calls the "3 Cs: Convince, Collaborate and Create" you will learn how to motivate people to help you achieve your ends.

Hispanic Trends Magazine

UP

Influence, Power
And
The U Perspective
The Art of Getting What You Want

by
Lee E. Miller
with
Barbara Jackson

Edited by Stephanie St. Pierre, MDiv, MPH

Your Career Doctors Press

Morristown NJ
Singapore

Library of Congress Cataloging-in-Publication Data

Miller, Lee E.

UP Influence, Power and the U Perspective — The
Art of Getting what You Want / by Lee E. Miller
with Barbara Jackson

p. cm.

Includes index

ISBN-10: 0-9788355-0-6 (alk. paper)
ISBN-13: 978-0-9788355-0-7

1. Influence. 2 Psychology. 3. Negotiation. I Jackson,
Barbara II Title

BF637.N4 M55   2007

158'.5'082-dc-dc21   2006907549

852 − 7541

Your Career Doctors
Press

ISBN-10: 0-9788355-0-6

ISBN-13: 978-0-9788355-0-7

Table of Contents

Introduction

The important thing is what you cause others to do rather than what you do yourself.

Terry Leah, CEO Tesco

Are You On Your Way UP?

What would you give to be able to get anyone to do whatever you wanted them to do? How different would your life be if you knew the secret for getting your boss, your co-workers, your employees, your children and your spouse to help you with whatever you need? What if you knew how to make your customers buy more products and not argue with you about the price? Harnessing the power of the U Perspective will make all that and more possible!

I love movies. They have a way of helping me to crystallize complex ideas and to express them in ways that are readily understandable. In one such movie, *Automobiles*, an alien scout on a reconnaissance mission to Earth reports back to his home planet describing what he has learned: "Earth is a planet run by four-wheel vehicles called automobiles. Each automobile has a human slave. Every day the human slave takes the automobile to a club where it spends all day socializing with other automobiles, while the human slave works in order to be able to house, feed and take care of the automobile."

The alien described exactly what he saw. It was accurate from his point of view. The movie illustrates the idea that everyone sees the world through the prism of their own upbringing, culture, experiences and values. Two people can look at the same thing, yet each sees something very different. Since we interact with others all the time, a better understanding of how they view things will make those interactions less confusing. For example, getting things done usually requires the help of others. The key to getting others to work with you is to learn to look "UP" and see the world the way they see it - through their U Perspective.

After graduating Harvard Law School, I practiced law for a number of years. I have spent most of my professional life though, in corporate America, first as the Vice President of Labor and Employee Relations for Macys and then as the Senior Vice President of Human Resources for Barneys New York, USA Networks and TV Guide, running their human resources departments. In those jobs I experienced stock market booms, the bursting of the dotcom bubble, leveraged buyouts, mergers, acquisitions, bankruptcies and restructurings. Throughout it all the one thing that was critical to my success was my ability to influence others - to get people to want to help me.

During the last six years as the Managing Director of NegotiationPlus.com I have worked with individuals and organizations such as the National Basketball Association, Bank of America, Citigroup, Glaxo-

SmithKline, Novartis, Toyota and Grey Advertising as a trainer, consultant and coach to help employees learn how to more effectively influence others. As an adjunct professor at Seton Hall I have taught Managerial Negotiating to MBA students. I have also written a book with my daughter, *A Woman's Guide to Successful Negotiating* which was selected as one of the fifty best books for professional women by Atlanta Women magazine and was featured on "The Early Show" and "Good Morning America." In the process I have had the opportunity to reflect on my own experiences as well as on those of other executives that I have worked with, trained and interviewed. I have also benefited from the insights of my co-host on the "Your Career Doctors" Radio Show, Barbara Jackson, the former Director of the Office of Management and Budget for the Commonwealth of Massachusetts, and someone who has held several posts under New York City Mayor Ed Koch, including Commissioner of Surface Transit and First Deputy Commissioner of the City Ports Department. Barbara, now a successful entrepreneur in her own right, has shared her experiences influencing others and has helped me to write this book.

Out of all these experiences and reflections came the concept of the U Perspective. When people first hear me talk about the U Perspective they say, "I know what that means – what I'd do if I were you, right?" Wrong! That's the "Me" Perspective. The U Perspective means what you will do precisely because you are YOU! Your personal experiences, background, likes and desires, what happened to you previously in similar circumstances, all will determine how you size up a particular situation. Your U Perspective determines how you will react and what you will do. It is as unique as your signature and when I understand your U Perspective I can predict your next move with certainty. I can craft my responses in ways that not only make you do what I want but satisfy your needs and aspirations as well. It's like being a fortune teller or a great coach who can anticipate what is going to happen next on the field and always seems to be one step ahead of the other team.

Here's an example of how the U Perspective works. Several years ago, my friend Ted had an opportunity to take a great job, but it would have required him to move to Washington, D.C. His elderly parents were rapidly approaching the time when they would need his help in order to continue to live independently. The job offer posed a real dilemma for him. He was excited about the opportunity but it would require him to move away from his parents. As an only child Ted wanted to live close enough to be readily accessible to his aging parents if they needed something.

Ted and I have been close friends for over twenty years, so, of course, we had numerous discussions as he wrestled with his decision. My advice went something like this: "Well, it's a job you would love, that's for sure, but I've lived in Washington and I know you would hate the heat and humidity. Washington in August is like nothing you've ever experienced. Besides, you love doing things with your dad. You'd miss that. And you would really feel guilty if either of your parents got sick and you weren't there to help."

My advice was different than the advice he was getting from his neighbor, who was also a good friend.

His neighbor's advice was more along these lines: "If I were you, here's what I'd do in this situation. I'd take the job and find a housekeeper who would be willing to drive your parents to the store and to the doctor. Then I'd buy discount airline tickets in advance so I could afford to visit frequently. That way you could take the job you want and still make sure your parents were okay." His neighbor even printed out a flight schedule from the internet to show Ted how easy it would be.

Both of us gave Ted good advice. The difference is that I was trying to look at things from Ted's point of view - what was important to him. I carefully avoided telling him what I would do given the same opportunity. His neighbor based his advice to Ted on what he would do if he found himself in a similar situation. Both suggestions were reasonable. Both solved the problem of how Ted could be sure his parents received the assistance they needed. But only one approach was based on what was important to Ted - his U Perspective - and only that was truly helpful to Ted in making his decision.

During my conversations with Ted what I really wanted to know was what was going to be best for Ted, given his past history, his values, his beliefs and his motivators? What would make him happy? Ted asked me many times, "What would you do?" He may even have said, "What would you do if you were me?" I recognized that those were the wrong questions to ask. It didn't matter what I would do. I have a brother and sister. My parents are a lot younger than Ted's parents. I had never lived less than a couple of hours drive from my parents. I'm not their primary backup when they need help. What I would do if I faced the same type of choice wasn't relevant for Ted's decision. I tried to figure out what would make Ted happiest based on what I knew of his past behavior and what was important to him. I sought to understand Ted's U Perspective. Ted's neighbor relied on his own values to advise Ted - what he would do if he were offered a great job that required him to relocate. Ted's neighbor focused on himself, his Me Perspective, not Ted's U Perspective. While his advice was sound, it was not the right advice for Ted.

Let's suppose for a second, that instead of giving Ted advice, each of us was trying to influence Ted's decision. Who would have been more effective? The friend who came at Ted's dilemma from his own point of view or me trying to understand what Ted's natural inclinations were and suggesting arguments, and alternatives, that might encourage Ted to make the decision I favored. For example, if I were a recruiter trying to get Ted to accept the job in Washington, D.C., understanding his U Perspective might have led me to suggest that Ted relocate his parents along with himself. To entice Ted to accept the position perhaps I could even have convinced the prospective employer to pay some of Ted's parents' relocation costs rather than simply offering Ted more money.

That is the beauty of the U Perspective. Like jujitsu, which redirects the force aimed by your adversary at you and uses it against him or her, understanding how someone else sees a situation allows you to harness the power of that person's values and to redirect their behavior in a way that satisfies your interests, as well as theirs. Once you take the time and effort to understand someone, you know what motivates them. That allows you not only to predict what they are likely to do, but also to affect their behavior. If I correctly understand your U Perspective and operate from it, I will be in sync with what you are thinking and therefore will be able to influence your actions. Your point of view - your U Perspective - lets me know what you need and want. If I can provide that to you in a way that suits my needs, I can create a mutually beneficial solution. In negotiating or sales terms, this is a win/win solution. In leadership terms it is how you gain buy-in from your employees. In reality it is better than either of these concepts. Everyone's values are respected and solutions are found that are expressly suited to each individual's wants and needs. Agreements last and everybody feels good about the interaction.

Negotiating is one area where understanding how to apply this concept will provide immediate dividends. However, there is nothing easy about discovering your negotiating partner's U Perspective. Take the example of Ted's neighbor. Yes, the same neighbor who advised Ted to take the job in Washington, D.C. Soon after Ted turned the job down his neighbor decided to accept a position in another city and as a result needed to sell his home. The very first week the house was on the market the neighbor received an offer at his admittedly high asking price, but to everyone's amazement he turned the offer down.

He turned the offer down because the buyers wanted him to agree to replace the roof at his expense before they would agree to enter into a contract. While the neighbor agreed that the roof needed to be replaced he felt that he had taken that into account when he priced the house. So he turned down the offer, assuming the prospective buyers would come back with a slightly lower counter-offer and fix the roof themselves after they moved in. That did not happen. There was no counter-offer and, in order to start his new job, the neighbor ended up having to move before he could sell the house. After paying two mortgages for a few months, he lowered his asking price and was finally able to sell the house. As it turned out, he would have been better off if he'd accepted the first buyers' offer and simply replaced the roof as they had requested.

Interestingly, the family who made the initial offer ended up buying another home in the neighborhood and I subsequently met them. I asked them about their dealings with Ted's neighbor. It turns out that they'd had a really bad experience with a home renovation project previously and absolutely did not want to tackle another one at the same time they were starting new jobs and relocating their family. They really liked Ted's neighbor's house and would even have been willing to increase their offer slightly but they didn't want to have to oversee the work on the roof. Ted's neighbor just assumed that the potential buyers were using the roof as leverage to negotiate a lower price, what he would have done in their situation, and never bothered to find out what their actual U Perspective was - to buy a home in move-in condition. As a result, Ted's neighbor lost out on a great opportunity. He could have gotten a better deal and sold his home six months earlier had he only taken the time to discover the buyers' U Perspective.

The U Perspective applies to all your dealings with people. If you want to get a friend to go with you to a movie that you really want to see, but which he is only lukewarm about, find a theater where the movie is playing near your friend's favorite restaurant. Then suggest that you have dinner at the restaurant first. If you want to inspire the employees that work for you, seek to motivate them in terms of what they care about - their U Perspective.

Knowing how to use the U Perspective will enable you to take control of situations and to influence events. It will reduce aggravation and stress in your life. It will empower you. This concept is easy to articulate but most people don't really understand what it means or how to go about discovering how someone else sees the world. This book explores how to do that in your daily life as well as in the major business activities that you undertake.

Unleashing the power of the U Perspective requires you to look at the world differently. Learning to see situations through the eyes of others will enable you to get what you want in every aspect of your life. Whether you are leading others, negotiating deals, selling to customers, providing customer service, working with other departments, recruiting candidates or dealing with your spouse, your friends or your children, ultimately your success depends on gaining their cooperation and getting them to do what you want. Understanding how to read someone's U Perspective will allow you to do just that. That's the power of UP.

Part One:
Which Way Is UP?

Chapter 1

We don't see things as they are. We see things as we are.

Anais Nin

What Is The U Perspective?

Kitty Van Bortel built one of the largest Subaru dealerships in the country by recognizing that most women disliked the way cars traditionally were sold. That realization came to her one evening while she was watching Larry King broadcasting from the Detroit auto show. He was interviewing CEOs from what were then referred to as the "Big Three" U.S. auto companies - Ford, GM and Chrysler. A woman called in and said, "I don't understand why I have to fight for a good price when I go to a dealership." One of the CEOs responded "Most people like to negotiate. It's fun." The others readily agreed. All three CEOs shared a belief that the majority of customers liked to negotiate and that anyone who did not was an oddity. They accepted this view without ever questioning its validity because they liked to negotiate and most of the people they knew - automobile executives and dealers - liked to negotiate. To them negotiating was an essential and enjoyable part of the car buying experience. They could not imagine selling cars any other way.

Kitty understood that many customers, particularly women, did not like to negotiate. So she created a dealership catering to women where they didn't have to negotiate. Kitty understood the U Perspective of the women she was seeking as customers. They wanted to be treated with respect and they did not want to have to negotiate price when they purchased a car. On the other hand, the CEOs of the major U.S. automobile manufacturers at the time simply assumed that everyone saw the world the same way they did, at least when it came to buying a car. As a result, they missed a major business opportunity. Since most individuals surround themselves with people who think the same way they do, the inability to see things through the eyes of those who view the world differently is a critical blind spot shared by most people. Kitty's idea proved so successful that General Motors subsequently adopted that approach when it launched its Saturn line.

This story illustrates how failing to understand the U Perspective of others can mean the loss of sales, the loss of customers and countless lost business opportunities. In your personal life, it can result in misunderstandings, unnecessary arguments and problems with children, spouses, friends and co-workers. As long as we believe that others see the world the same way that we do we will continue to misunderstand why customers don't buy from us, why people don't respond to us the way we expect them to and why our children don't do as we ask.

Most people view the world based on their own points

of reference that are derived from their personal experiences and those of the people close to them. For example, why would a professional quarterback, like Ben Roethlisberger, making tens of millions of dollars a year, risk his career by riding a motorcycle without a helmet? Obviously, Ben enjoys riding motorcycles and he enjoys this experience more without the restrictions of a helmet. Moreover, he believes that his skill and dexterity as an elite athlete give him a greater ability than the average rider to safely maneuver his bike. Because he has done so previously without incident, after a while he actually starts to believe that, for him, there is no real risk in doing so. While he probably would concede that statistically riding a motorcycle without a helmet is risky, based on his own history he doesn't believe that those statistics apply to him and he shouldn't have to compromise his enjoyment by wearing a helmet. Reasoning with him would not convince him otherwise because his personal experience is to the contrary.

That was his U Perspective and no amount of persuasion or logic could change it. Once you accept that, you understand that getting him not to engage in that behavior requires another type of persuasion beyond simply reasoning with him, such as including a provision in his contract prohibiting the riding of a motorcycle. One day Ben had a near career ending motorcycle accident. His U Perspective was immediately altered – the statistics and logic remained the same but because his own experience changed, so did his U Perspective.

Since everyone has had different life experiences, you are likely to view the world very differently from many of the people with whom you have occasion to interact. There is a scene in the movie *Annie Hall* which aptly illustrates this basic human tendency. The character played by Woody Allen in the movie is in therapy with his girlfriend. He complains to their counselor that they hardly ever have sex. His girlfriend denies that, stating that they are constantly having sex. When the counselor asks them specifically how often they have sex, they respond in unison, "three times a week."

Since our beliefs and values are developed over time, on a subconscious level, most people simply assume that everyone sees the world the way they do. Even when we recognize that someone else sees a situation differently than we do, our first instinct usually is to try to persuade them to see things our way. The U Perspective takes the opposite approach. Its effectiveness is not rooted in the ability to convince others to change their views or adopt different values. Instead, its power comes from recognizing what others already believe and want and providing solutions based on that information. The U Perspective allows you to get what you want by working with another person's belief system, not challenging it. To achieve this level of understanding, you need to discover how the person you are trying to influence perceives a situation and what is important to him or her - to learn to see things through their eyes. Once you understand how they see a situation you have the ability to construct, and present, options in a way that more effectively influences what they do.

Whenever I describe the U Perspective to people, I receive knowing looks and nods. My audiences think they have already mastered this skill because they are customer-focused, use consultative selling techniques, employ win/win negotiating tactics or practice values-based leadership. To be sure, all of these practices require an element of understanding others. To most people, however, that means trying to figure out what they would do "if they were in the other person's shoes." In fact, some well-known authors use those very words when they give advice to their readers as to how they should go about exerting influence.

Thinking in those terms undermines much of the otherwise good advice offered by these writers because they are starting from an erroneous premise. That approach assumes that everyone has the same needs and desires and that those needs and desires can be objectively discerned, if only one properly analyzes the situation. Assuming others will behave as you would in a given situation is doubly problematic because it provides a false sense that you understand someone else's motivations, thereby keeping you from making the necessary effort to actually find out what will influence that person's behavior. People do not want you to treat them the way you want to be treated. They want to be treated the way they want to be treated.

For example, you may be logical while the person you are seeking to influence reacts emotionally. The conventional wisdom is to try to remove emotions from the situation while you attempt to craft a mutually acceptable solution. That may work if the emotion is temporary and the people you are trying to influence generally share your U Perspective. But, what if they do not share your culture, your background or your predispositions? Will you be able to persuade them with logic, or would it be better to try to satisfy their emotional needs at that moment? The U Perspective focuses on what motivates an individual to make decisions. If you can determine that before you try to influence someone you have a better chance of presenting options that will persuade.

Understanding a person's U Perspective means being able to predict what they will do because they are who they are - given how they have behaved in the past and how they see the situation confronting them. The key to doing that is to determine what they value and what motivates them. Different people are motivated by different things. They may be motivated by money, power, status, time, a desire to attract a partner, ease and comfort, wanting to help others, a sense of fairness, teamwork, family, friendship, recognition and/or challenge. Even a desire for fame can be a major motivator for some people. What motivates each of us is different depending on the situation and the other people involved.

The following story illustrates the importance of quickly determining the U Perspective of the person you want to influence. A fast food restaurant chain was seeking to have a well known singer do a promotion for them. The singer was already well established and did not need the publicity. To entice him to do the promotion the chain offered him a large sum of money. He declined. In response, the chain put even more money on the table. Once again he turned them down. Finally someone from the chain did some research to find out what else might motivate the singer, since money didn't seem to be getting them where they wanted to go. They discovered that this singer was heavily involved with promoting a certain charity so they restructured the offer to satisfy his U Perspective. For every one of his CDs they gave away as part of the promotion, the company would donate a certain amount of money to the singer's chosen charity. That way the promotion was consistent with how he saw himself and the image he wanted to portray to the world.

In the end, the chain got the singer, but they did so at a high price. Having previously offered to pay him a significant fee to do this promotion the company was stuck. The singer was not willing to accept a lower fee now just because they had also offered to make a donation to his favorite charity. So the chain paid the singer and they donated to the charity. Unknown to the company was the fact that the singer felt that being identified with a fast food chain would damage the image he had worked so hard to cultivate for himself. By structuring the promotion as an opportunity for the singer to benefit a worthwhile cause, the company was able to remove any issue he otherwise would have had about how promoting a fast food chain might impact his image. If they had understood the singer's U Perspective early on, and presented the idea of the charitable donation from the outset, the singer would have probably agreed to participate in the promotion for a lot less money.

A person's U Perspective is not only individual to them but will change as their circumstances change. While money can effectively be used as a motivator, even money becomes a substantially less useful motivator once you achieve a certain level of wealth. There is a significant body of research that shows that once personal wealth reaches a certain level additional wealth produces virtually no increase in one's sense of happiness. Moreover, according to Richard Layard, a professor at the London School of Economics peoples' sense of their own wealth is subjective and is determined primarily by comparing themselves to others. Therefore when incomes rise across a nation there is no greater sense of wealth or happiness. For example, real income in Japan more than quintupled over the thirty years starting in the 1950s yet researchers found no corresponding increase in how happy people felt. Even very wealthy people can feel disadvantaged when their friends are significantly wealthier than they are. Understanding that may cause you to propose a business opportunity to a very wealthy individual by focusing on some other benefit beyond just its profitability, such as by making it exclusively available to that individual or by allowing that individual to gain status by being able to offer it to his or her friends.

Taking advantage of someone's U Perspective not only requires understanding how someone else sees a given situation, and what might motivate them, but also requires not being judgmental. While intellectually we can accept that others may see things differently than we do, it is human nature to believe that views differing from our own are less valid. This leads to ineffective and often counterproductive efforts to get people to change their U Perspectives. We assume that those who see a situation differently than we do simply do not have as much, or as accurate, information as we have. We believe that if only we provide more information or explain our position more clearly, we can change their mind. Taking advantage of the U Perspective also requires getting past our assumption that we know what motivates others - i.e. the same things that motivate us.

We automatically assume that in proposing a business deal the key is to demonstrate that the deal will be profitable. Because that is typically the case, people fail to recognize that there are instances where that will not be sufficient to persuade someone to enter into a specific deal. Tamar Simon Hoff, a Hollywood producer, director and writer recognized this when she was trying to convince a wealthy businessman to invest in a movie she was producing. After initially being turned down she took a different approach, keeping in mind that his son was studying filmmaking. She put forward a new proposal that she knew he would not be able to resist; she offered the investor's son his first movie job. Because the deal, while financially sound, was too small to interest this particular investor, she had to rethink how to get his attention, and his investment, by appealing to a different aspect of his U Perspective - his son's future. That was much more valuable to him than the profit he would eventually make from the film. This time he said yes to the deal.

Once you discover someone's U Perspective, influencing that person's behavior is a fairly simple matter. Unleashing the power of the U Perspective requires reconciling two concepts which at first glance may seem contradictory. The first is that two people looking at the same situation can see it completely differently and neither need be wrong. The second is that, although a person may unequivocally view a situation in a certain way, there may be multiple ways to satisfy that person's U Perspective. Once you accept other people's desires and values in a non-judgmental way, you can explore ways to satisfy them. As there will be many possible means of doing so you will be able to focus on satisfying them in ways that enable you to achieve your objectives as well. Using the U Perspective does not require that you share someone else's values, only that you learn to see them and consider them. It provides a way of dealing successfully with others and gaining what you want in a variety of different contexts.

It is extremely difficult to change anyone's U Perspective. Fortunately, you don't need to do so to effectively influence their behavior. What you may need to change is your approach; in the end that is the only part of the influencing equation that you have total control over. This doesn't mean that if you are working with someone who believes that there is nothing inherently wrong with lying, you should allow them to lie. Rather it accepts the fact that you are dealing with a person who will lie unless you recognize their U Perspective and respond accordingly. You could try to change a liar's U Perspective by attempting to convince him that lying is morally wrong, an approach that is unlikely to work. Or, you could appeal to another value that is part of the liar's U Perspective - fear - by showing that if he lies he may get caught or you will be compelled to report his misconduct. If you could suggest a way for him to achieve his objectives without lying, you could change his behavior without having to change his U Perspective.

A person's U Perspective may appear to change as circumstances change. However, it is more likely that their U Perspective has remained the same while the changed circumstances give rise to their U Perspective being expressed differently. For instance, when Barbara Jackson was Budget Director for the Commonwealth of Massachusetts, she worked with the head of the National Governor's Association, Governor Bill Clinton. One of the major issues that the Association was promoting was an end to unfunded mandates - obligations that Federal legislation places on states without providing funding to pay for them. After Governor Clinton was elected President, in his farewell letter to the National Governors Association, he reiterated his position opposing unfunded mandates from the Federal government. Yet, after he was inaugurated and assumed the role of President, the very first piece of legislation that he signed was an unfunded mandate. When questioned about this by a representative of the National Governors Association, President Clinton said, "I know that I said I would not support unfunded mandates but I needed to sign this bill to appease Congress."

No one has ever accused President Clinton of needing to be consistent. However, his U Perspective really hadn't changed at all. It had always been based on doing what he deemed necessary to further his agenda. As a governor he needed to garner the support of his fellow governors and took a strong stand against unfunded mandates. As President his fellow governors were no longer his top priority. His primary concern had become working with Congress in order to get legislation passed.

Ultimately, a person's U Perspective is what motivates them in a given instance. While a person's core values may not change, how those values play out will vary as his or her circumstances change. Recognizing this will enable you to predict and thereby influence their behavior.

The difference between getting what you want and walking away empty handed often depends on how well you comprehend someone else's U Perspective. So why do people so often ignore the U Perspectives of those they are trying to influence? In part this results from the common misconception, discussed previously, that all we need to do when seeking to influence others is to determine what would influence us in a similar situation. However even after people realize the need to understand what motivates those they seek to influence, most people do not know how to determine what motivates someone else. Nor have they learned how to leverage those motivators in order to induce others to help them achieve their own objectives.

When I was at Harvard Law School I took a course on negotiating from one of the foremost experts on that topic in the nation. Negotiating is a basic form of influencing that is used in almost every situation where you seek to gain the cooperation of others. Research on negotiating provides critical insights into how we can more effectively influence others. I have subsequently taken other courses and done extensive reading on the subjects of negotiating and influencing. Much of what I have learned involves various tips and assorted strategies designed to persuade others to do what you want in specific situations. Some experts in the field have sought to go beyond that and to develop a systematic way of looking at negotiating and influencing. I share their belief that to be consistently successful in your efforts to influence others requires a systematic approach to the subject. However, most efforts to develop such an approach have lacked flexibility because they assume there is one best way to go about influencing others. So while the proffered approach might be effective in a variety of situations it does not necessarily work in others.

There is no one right way to exert influence. The best approach depends on who we are seeking to influence and the circumstances in which we seek to exert that influence. As we have seen, how best to approach someone depends on that person's U Perspective. There are, however, specific methods that you can learn that will enable you to be more effective when you interact with others and that will enhance your ability to do so.

The Convince, Collaborate and Create (3 Cs) Influencing Method that I developed came out of my realization that while you need to use a systematic influencing approach to consistently achieve the best results in your dealings with others, there is no single approach that works in every situation. Sometimes the best way to influence someone is by appealing to their emotions, at other times it may be best to appeal to their objective interests and sometimes, to get what you want, it is necessary to change how you structure your interactions with that person. At times you will need to do all three. Each of these approaches is different, yet each can, when applied in the right way, affect what someone does. The 3 Cs Influencing Method combines each of these approaches into a methodology that can be applied in a systematic way. This method consists of a three part formula to win others over - one part psychology, one part problem solving and one part structuring your interactions for maximum impact.

Convince harnesses emotions to affect behavior. It relies on the psychology of persuasion to enhance the perceived value of what is being offered. It employs the U Perspective to focus on what others already care about by emphasizing the common ground between that and what you are proposing. These techniques draw on the study of rhetoric, game theory, heuristics and body language. The specific influencing tools that one can use as part of the Convince approach are: anchoring, legitimacy, active listening, purposeful questioning, and the rhetorical skills needed to most effectively deliver a message.

Collaborate is a rational interest-based model of influencing that draws from organizational theory and win/win negotiating. It employs a problem solving approach that seeks to rationally determine how the parties can best work together to achieve a common goal that will maximize everyone's interests. Collaborate uses the relationship between the parties to encourage them to work together to achieve mutual gains. In so doing, the parties can actually increase the value of what is available to them. The specific tools we use when we Collaborate are: developing relationships, leveraging relationships, determining interests, problem-solving and taking advantage of value differences.

Create works on the theory that how you structure your interactions with others affects the substantive outcome of those interactions. It requires taking a fresh look at how you interact with others. Create takes advantage of the fact that individuals typically have a much greater ability to control how they structure their dealings with others than they realize. The specific tools that we use when we Create are examining assumptions, exploring alternatives, changing the people involved, trying different things and creating new paradigms.

Each approach harnesses the power of the U Perspective in a different way. These approaches are not employed sequentially but are used simultaneously depending on the situation and the particular people involved. Each approach offers a different, but complimentary, method of gaining the cooperation and support of others.

The 3 Cs Influencing Method can be used with people on a one-on-one basis, as you might do when you sell, negotiate or deal with customers. These principles can also be applied to your personal life when you are dealing with your children, your friends or your significant other. This methodology works equally well as a leadership model to exert influence throughout an organization. In Part 1 of this book, I discuss the role the U Perspective plays in the 3 Cs Influencing Method. I will also discuss how to use this model in the context of cross-cultural influencing and negotiating. Part 2 of this book focuses on the general principles used to Convince, Collaborate and Create. In Part 3, I apply these principles in specific contexts such as negotiating, delivering customer service, managing people and recruiting, as well as how to use them to advance your own career. Initially my focus will be on how this method can be applied when we seek to influence individuals on a one-on-one basis. I conclude by discussing the elusive concept of leadership and how the 3 Cs Influencing Method can be used to influence groups and to lead organizations.

Chapter 2

The best way to persuade others is with you
- by listening to them.

Dean Rusk

Discovering The U Perspective In Others

When Claire Irving was a Managing Director of Kroll Investigations, one of the largest private investigating firms in the country, she was given the unenviable task of trying to collect in excess of four million dollars in outstanding bills owed to the firm, all of which were several years old. Yet she was able to collect $3.98 million dollars, approximately 98% of those bills. How did she do it? Simply by asking the right questions and listening to the answers. Claire called each of the clients that owed the firm money to find out why they had not paid. Once she determined what the client's U Perspective was she knew what had to be done to get them to pay. Usually the problem was something that the firm had done wrong or had promised to do but hadn't. By listening and allowing the client to feel that they had been heard, in almost every case, Claire was able to get the client to pay. There was no need to negotiate;

all she had to do was resolve the problem as the client perceived it to be. In other words, she satisfied their U Perspective. Once she did that, payment followed.

The power of the U Perspective comes from being able to get inside someone else's head to find out what makes them tick. As we have seen, two people can look at the same situation and perceive it in totally different ways. That can occur, in part, because different people focus on different things and, in part, because each interprets what they see through the prism of their own life experiences and personal values. The prism through which people evaluate what they see is their U Perspective. To discover what someone's U Perspective is you must become an expert listener.

BE A GOOD LISTENER

Good listeners are observant. The best listener that I ever met was a New York City police detective. John pays attention to everything. He hears not only what you say, but also what you don't say. He watches your every movement and expression. He is aware of your body language. He takes note of your clothes and your mode of transportation. He is not only aware of who your friends are but hears what they have to say as well. He makes you feel comfortable and gets you to open up to him. In five minutes John usually knows things about you that even your best friend doesn't know. He is like a giant hearing aid turned up to the maximum volume for the purpose of discovering peoples' U Perspectives. As a result he has a remarkable success rate. To this day, I try to emulate his ability to use all his senses in order to listen more effectively.

Well, John's a cop, so his job depends on having great listening skills. If you aren't a police officer, why should you emulate John? Because being a good listener is the key to determining a person's U Perspective and that is invaluable information that can be used in almost any situation. Good listeners like John share certain characteristics that are relatively easy to learn.

Good listeners make people feel comfortable. Nancy Erika Smith, an employment lawyer who has both tried and settled multi-million dollar cases, always makes sure everyone feels comfortable before she begins settlement discussions. Nancy attempts to put people at ease. She makes certain the room is at the right temperature, puts food and coffee out, and thanks everyone for coming. She wants people to feel free to open up to her.

What makes people feel comfortable, however, differs from person to person. Feelings of comfort are often subtle. They occur not only on a conscious but on a subliminal level as well, making the little things you do important. Find out what you need to do to make someone comfortable. For example, you might call a person's assistant to ask what their boss likes to drink and have it available when they arrive. If food is going to be served find out what the people you are meeting with like and, equally important, what they dislike. Create a sense of belonging. Public relations firms often display pictures of their clients so that when prospective clients visit, they feel like they belong there among their peers.

Good listeners are courteous. If you want to find

out what someone cares about start by being polite. Let other people talk. Don't interrupt. Allow others to finish what they are saying before you respond. Acknowledge that you have heard what is being said by smiling and nodding. Good manners are always appropriate and people respond positively to them. Treat people courteously and they will open up to you like you were a long lost friend.

Good listeners stay focused. Concentrate completely on the other person. Be aware of everything - not only what someone says but what they do as well. Eliminate distractions. Normally after a few minutes our minds start to wander so it is important to block out distracting thoughts. Avoid thinking about how you are going to respond. Just pay close attention to what is being said. Not only will you gain valuable information but the person you are speaking with will feel that you really care about what they are saying.

Good listeners seek to listen more than they speak. Most people love to talk. So the less you speak the more information you will garner. Allow for pauses in the conversation. Don't feel that you have to speak whenever someone stops to collect their thoughts or is contemplating what to do or say next. They may be on the verge of providing you with the information you are seeking. Allow them the opportunity to do so and wait until you are certain that they have finished speaking before you reply.

Good listeners don't rely on memory alone. Take notes whenever possible. Write important things down. If note-taking during a meeting would not be appropriate, jot down your recollection of what was said as soon as you leave the meeting. Studies show that we forget 50% of what we hear after 8 hours and 95% of what we hear within two days.

Good listeners care. The most important part of being a good listener is to truly care about what someone is saying. People can tell when you are sincere and when you are not. If you try to understand how someone else sees things because you are truly interested in their point of view, they will know it and will be more open about their needs and concerns. Being genuinely concerned is what makes a person an effective listener.

If you fail to listen well, you are likely to misread the U Perspective of others and that can lead to disastrous results. Barbara Jackson relayed one such near disaster to me that she was able to avert by recognizing and seeking to satisfy the U Perspectives of an entire audience, as well as that of the person who hired her to speak. Barbara was asked to speak at a conference at the last minute. Since she had very little time to prepare, she agreed on the condition that she be allowed to use a speech that she had previously delivered at a different conference. Her topic wasn't the conference planner's first choice, but he was in a jam. Barbara asked him three times if he could live with her chosen topic. He agreed and the title of the talk she was going to deliver was even included in the contract. Barbara couldn't have been clearer about what she was going to talk about. But the conference organizer was too busy to listen. Barbara had agreed to do a speech. It filled the sixty minute opening he had to fill, she had the right credentials and the topic dealt with public finance. So the conference organizer signed the contract and even paid her in advance. You would think the problem was solved and Barbara had come up with a win/win solution. Unfortunately, as it turned out, that was not the case.

When she got to the conference, Barbara looked at the brochure and, to her dismay, next to her name was the original topic the conference planner had wanted her to address. Barbara had to speak for an hour to a group of people who thought they were coming to hear a talk on "Working with Wall Street Rating Agencies" and were about to get a speech on "Performance Based Budgeting."

From Barbara's perspective what did it matter? She'd already been paid and could rightfully place the blame on the conference organizer for the mix up. However, that would have disregarded the U Perspective of the audience and that of the conference organizer. Regardless of who was to blame, the audience would not be happy if they had to listen to a speech on a topic they hadn't signed up for and weren't interested in. What about the conference organizer's U Perspective? He was influential in the industry and was held in high regard by most people in the audience. Moreover, he was Barbara's friend. How would he feel if she truthfully shared with the audience what had actually happened?

So what did Barbara do? She sought to determine the audience's U Perspective. She told them that there had been a mix up and that her prepared speech and her slides were on the topic of "Performance Based Budgeting." She offered the audience a choice. She could give her prepared speech or they could engage in an informal give and take discussion about rating agencies. Guess what they opted for? They had a lively discussion about the rating process. As it turned out, the audience rated the informal program as one of the best conference sessions and several people from the audience subsequently hired Barbara to do work for them. Being cognizant of the audience's U Perspective allowed Barbara to turn a potential disaster into a positive experience for everyone. And, as a result of taking into account the conference organizer's U Perspective, they remain good friends to this day and he has been helpful to her on many subsequent occasions.

ACTIVE LISTENING

It is not enough just to be a good listener; you need to be an active listener. Active listening techniques are designed to encourage people to talk and to tell you what they really care about. One way to do that is to ask lots of questions. But there are other active listening techniques that you can learn as well. These techniques will get people to open up to you and to reveal information that more clearly illuminates their U Perspectives.

Active listening is the process of encouraging someone to engage in conversation. (It is also an important part of the 3 Cs Influencing Method which we will discuss in more detail in the next few chapters.) There are several basic active listening techniques: attending, reflecting back, clarifying, encouraging, recognizing feelings, using silence and summarizing. Each of these techniques will help you gather information that will assist you in learning what people care about and how to motivate them to want to help you.

Attending. This technique consists of demonstrating your interest through your body language, facial expressions and gestures in order to encourage someone to continue speaking. There are many ways that you can use body language to show interest. Sit or stand directly facing the person you are speaking with while maintaining an open posture. Lean forward. Look the person in the eye. Nod your head and smile. Attending can be used by itself or in conjunction with other active listening techniques.

Reflecting back. Reflecting back is paraphrasing, or putting into your own words, your understanding of what has been said to you. This technique is particularly useful if you are uncertain about what someone is saying. Paraphrasing enables you to determine whether or not you have accurately understood what was said and it encourages the speaker to continue talking. Some phrases that can be used when you are reflecting back are: "So what you're saying is...," "Let me see if I understand correctly...," "In other words..." and "It sounds like..."

Clarifying. This technique is simply asking for more information when something is not clear or you want a better understanding of what has been said. "What do you mean by that?" is a typical clarifying question.

Encouraging. This technique uses encouraging comments to get someone to continue talking. In addition to non-verbal attending gestures such as nodding your head, smiling, leaning forward and looking someone in the eye, interject phases such as "I see," "Really?", "That's interesting" or even "Uh huh!" These phrases encourage people to tell you more about what they are thinking and how they are feeling. Encouraging can also involve more direct invitations to continue, such as "Tell me more," "Go on" or "I'd love to hear more about that."

Recognizing Feelings.   Feelings reveal critical aspects of what is important to a person. Saying things such as "I see you're angry" or "I am sorry this seems to be upsetting you" are ways you can bring someone's feelings out into the open. Simply asking someone how they feel about an issue may reveal something about their U Perspective. It is frequently necessary to deal with feelings such as anger or anxiety before one can get down to determining facts and developing solutions.

Using Silence. Sometimes in order to elicit more of a response from someone, the best thing to do is to simply pause and say nothing. If you wait a few seconds most people take this as a cue to fill the conversation gap. Most of us will say something, anything, just to fill the void. When you remain quiet people will usually continue talking and provide you with additional valuable information. Try this at home with your spouse or significant other. Ask a general question and then, after they respond, just remain silent and continue to look directly at them, smiling and nodding. Even if they appear to have finished speaking, after a brief pause, they will inevitably continue, elaborating on what they have already said. Using silence can be an especially effective way to elicit useful information.

Summarizing.   Use the summarizing technique when you want to make sure that you and the person with whom you are speaking understand what has been said or agreed upon. Summarize what was said and ask if your understanding is correct. This prevents misunderstandings and will help you gain insight into what the other person is thinking. Summarizing is also a good way to confirm that you have actually reached an agreement. It can also be used as a technique to close a sale. For example, if someone told you that they liked what you were proposing but they needed work completed by the end of next month for it to be worth pursuing, you could use the summarizing technique as a way of closing the sale by saying, "So, if I could guarantee you that we could complete the project by the end of next month, then everything else would be acceptable?"

LISTENING UNDER

Sometimes it's not enough to just hear what people are saying. At times you also have to read between the lines and hear what is not being said. I call this "listening under." Ellen Sandles is the Executive Director of the Tri-State Private Investors Network, an organization that showcases new business ventures to its members who are potential investors. She received a phone call from an investor who had been a guest at one of their recent meetings. Ellen had been hoping he would become a member of the group. However, he told her that while he enjoyed the meeting, he was not going to be able to join. Ellen realized that what he was saying was inconsistent with his behavior. People seldom call even once to say no to you. They wait for you to call them. This gentleman had made repeated attempts to call her before finally reaching her. So Ellen used her active listening skills and kept him talking until he finally told her what the real problem was. He wanted to play an active role in the companies in which he invested. Since all of the members he met at the meeting were passive investors, he was afraid that the group would see his desire to be involved in managing the companies that they invested in as a conflict of interest. Ellen assured him that they would not and, in fact, they would be happy to have one of their own members take an active role in watching over their investments. Ellen had to hear beyond the actual words he was saying in order to understand his U Perspective. Once she did Ellen had little difficulty persuading him to become a member.

Listening under often becomes necessary when people's actual U Perspective differs from the position they are expected to take in light of their position or the organization they are representing. People will ordinarily say what is expected of them but will behave in a manner consistent with their own U Perspective. Therefore, any time someone takes a position that is inconsistent with other information being conveyed to you through their behavior, they are probably not revealing their true U Perspective. That is a signal to delve deeper because unless you discover what they really care about you will not be able to achieve the results you are seeking.

Listening is the key to discovering someone's U Perspective. With practice anyone can become a good listener. But, remember just being a good listener is not always sufficient to discover what you need to do to motivate someone to want to help you. You have to be an active listener. Active listening techniques encourage people to talk, or talk more, and result in their telling you what they really care about. When someone's behavior is not consistent with their actions you have to listen harder and hear what they are not saying. The more someone talks and the more skillfully you listen, the more insight you will get into what is important to them and how they see things. You will understand their U Perspective and that is what you need to do if you are going to find effective ways to influence them and to reach long lasting agreements.

Chapter 3

A man's feet are planted in his country, but his eyes should survey the world.

George Santayana

The Cross-Cultural U Perspective

In Thailand the people are gracious and unfailingly polite. With a tropical climate and a Buddhist belief in reincarnation, they proceed at a slower pace than do Americans, Germans and Singaporeans. They place less importance on getting things done quickly than on avoiding conflict and ensuring that everyone is afforded the appropriate respect. That can lead to a myriad of miscommunications and hard feelings for foreigners who do not understand the U Perspective of their Thai counterparts. For example, an American businessman working in Thailand was constantly frustrated because his Thai partners repeatedly promised that they would meet certain agreed upon deadlines, but when those dates arrived the work was not completed. To the American businessman the Thais seemed like unreliable business partners repeatedly disrupting his plans and costing him money. Ultimately, the partnership broke down with bad feelings on both sides.

What went wrong? A mutual failure to understand each other had occurred. Had the businessman taken the time to understand his counterparts' U Perspectives, he would have recognized that when he asked his Thai partners if they could have a task done by a specific date their gracious nature guaranteed an affirmative response out of politeness and a desire to avoid conflict – two core Thai cultural values. In acquiescing to the businessman's requests, his Thai partners fully intended to try to meet his time deadlines, even though they knew that actually completing what was being asked of them in that time frame was not likely. With a different sense of time however, having done their best a Thai businessperson would feel that he or she had honored their part of the bargain even though the deadline was missed. In contrast, the results-oriented American would feel mislead and betrayed. The situation was further aggravated every time the businessman checked to see how the work was proceeding and was politely reassured that it was proceeding on schedule.

A better approach would have been for the businessman simply to ask his Thai partners when the requested tasks could be completed. Asking an open-ended question would have elicited a best estimate rather than an attempt to agree. Building in extra time for planning purposes and offering a bonus if the work was done more quickly, to take advantage of the Thai entrepreneurial spirit, wouldn't have hurt either.

While today's international businessmen and women might seem at first blush to share a common U Perspective, they are, nonetheless, products of their own cultures. Each country and regional subgroup has its own customs and unique way of life. Culture is a shared set of group values learned during our formative years through recurring social interactions which form patterns that are internalized by members of the group. Cultural norms are absorbed without people realizing it. They are deeply ingrained and often manifest themselves on a subconscious level. No one can avoid bringing their cultural assumptions, values, biases and ways of doing things along with them. That leads to "cultural blind spots" when we deal with someone from another country. Cultural blind spots are things we assume and simply take for granted which may be understood completely differently by someone that comes from another culture.

For example, I conduct exercises in my MBA Managerial Negotiating classes where my students negotiate with their classmates and are graded based on the outcomes of those negotiations. In one exercise students assume the roles of company and union representatives negotiating a collective bargaining agreement. Each side is given a score sheet explaining what their goals are and how many points achieving each is worth. In addition, each individual receives instructions explaining the U Perspective of the role they are playing with a separate sheet that explains how many bonus points the individual can earn if he or she achieves the personal objectives that are listed on that sheet. The students who do best in this particular exercise are those who maximize their team's score and still manage to achieve their personal goals.

In one instance, after the scores were tallied and the grades posted for this exercise, a Japanese student came up to speak with me. He was upset because he didn't receive a better grade. The student had achieved a good team score but in order to do so he had sacrificed his individual priorities. He felt that he should have received a higher grade because in his mind he had done well. Japanese culture expects an individual to subordinate his or her own personal interests for the good of the group. That is exactly what he had done.

When I designed this exercise, I failed to take into account my own U Perspective as an American. It never dawned on me that one of my students would believe that the proper way to negotiate would be to sacrifice his individual goals for the good of the group. Yet, even though the instructions specifically spelled out the importance of achieving each individual's personal objectives, my Japanese student's cultural upbringing instinctually took precedence over those instructions. I had fallen victim to my own cultural blind spot - the American view that individual success is paramount and can be achieved without sacrificing the interests of the organization for which you work. Understanding someone's cultural background is essential to understanding their U Perspective.

A good example of how cultural differences can impact the expectations of individuals from different backgrounds, even when they share a common goal, was brought home to me by two other students of mine - one Indian and one American. We were discussing the importance of customer service and how company rules and systems can get in the way of satisfying your customers. Both acknowledged that customer service was critical to a company's success. The American student took the position that it was each employee's responsibility to ensure that any reasonable request from the customer was satisfied. He argued that the employee, if necessary, should find a way around any rules that prevented good customer service. The Indian student, coming from a more process-driven and hierarchical society, took the position that the rules needed to be followed and that the employee was providing good customer service by handling the problem in accordance with company procedures. When challenged by the American student as to how someone could be providing good customer service if a problem was not solved to the customer's satisfaction the Indian student responded that determining how best to provide good customer service was a decision that was better made at a higher level. In his view it was management's role, not the employee's, to change the rules if they did not support good customer service.

To the American, the Indian student's U Perspective seemed not to sufficiently value good customer service. However, what the Indian student was really saying is that he believed management knew better than any single employee the best way to ensure good customer service and the rules they chose embodied those judgments. Respect for managerial experience and authority required that the employee not substitute his or her judgment for that of the employee's superiors. It is easy to see how these differing views as to the proper way to handle a customer problem could lead to frustrations and misunderstandings when American customers are dealing with Indian service providers. Once you understand the cultural U Perspective involved, it becomes clear that to impact the way customer service is provided in India requires focusing on systems and procedures.

How someone views time and relationships is also a significant aspect of their cultural U Perspective. To an American, time is a scarce and precious commodity like money. Hence the saying, time is money. Americans expect to begin their meetings on time, to stick to an agenda and to set and meet deadlines. In Japan, as in many other Eastern cultures, time is considered more fluid. Therefore if delays occur the Japanese accept this. Couple this view of time with the hierarchical nature of Japanese society and the need for decisions to be made by group consensus, and one can easily understand why deals take longer to complete there. To the same effect, the Chinese focus on ensuring that a job is done well, no matter how long it takes. The French and the Spanish require a relationship with the people they do business with. Time is the price they pay in order to develop and maintain that relationship.

Similarly in the Middle East, time is not as important as your relationship with the people with whom you are dealing. In the Middle East when you meet someone to discuss business it would be considered rude not to first discuss family and what is going on in their lives. The same is true when you speak by telephone. Social amenities always are expected to precede any business conversation, even if you have just spoken to the person a few minutes before. The ultimate signal that you have been accepted is being invited to a Middle Easterner's home - you are part of the family, so to speak. Not understanding that could be costly. For a woman doing business in that part of the world, getting to know someone's family can be helpful in being able to successfully conduct business with them. Whether you are a man or a woman, refusing an invitation to someone's home would be considered an insult that would likely preclude further business. Because of the importance Middle Easterner's place on their relationships with their business partners, what they refer to as "wasta," time spent developing relationships with potential business partners is usually time well spent.

In China, developing relationships with the right people can mean the difference between success and failure in your business endeavors. A friend who spent many years in China describes the difference between doing business in China and in the West as similar to the difference in how people date in those cultures. In the West, if you want to date someone you simply ask them out. If they are interested they will accept your invitation. In China, before you can date someone you first must win over their parents, uncles and aunts and the other important people in their life. So it is in business. If you want to do a deal in China you must first gain the support of the right people. If you don't, you can spend enormous amounts of time with your counterpart and not get anywhere. Who has influence over a particular transaction may not be readily apparent from someone's title. When doing business in China one needs to learn to navigate a matrix of relationships at all levels, introducing both subtleties and complexities to your dealings. So how do you know who are the right people to involve? There is only one way to find that out. Be diligent and do your research before you proceed. That, of course, takes time.

Similarly doing business in Latin America also requires taking the time to build a strong network of business relationships. It is important that you are personally endorsed by someone who is respected in the particular business environment where you are seeking to do business. However according to Maria Sastre, Vice President of Latin America and Asia Sales and Marketing for Royal Caribbean International, Latin America is not monolithic in terms of how time is viewed in different countries. "In Mexico, for example, you must be patient. It takes time to negotiate a successful business venture, the courting is more important than the engagement. In other countries such as Chile, they are much more prone to North American business dynamics, which are faster and involve less protocol."

None of these differing views of the relative importance of time and relationships is inherently right or wrong. They are just different. While the American view may lead to greater efficiency in getting deals done quickly, sometimes that creates more problems when deals are implemented. How do you measure the cost of constant pressure to do things better and faster in terms of quality as well as in terms of the health and well being of the individuals involved? Recognizing, not only that business transactions take longer, but also the reasons why they do, may enable you to speed up the process or, at least, to navigate it with greater success.

If your goal is to influence people who come from different cultural backgrounds it serves no useful purpose to denigrate their values. In fact, doing so is counterproductive because you are not going to change them. When you attack someone's cultural values they will resist with equal force. However, as in jujitsu where you redirect an attacker's force to avert their blows, if you accept someone's U Perspective in a non-judgmental way you can harness their values in order to help you further your goals. For example, Nadia Haridi, a human resources consultant with Right Management who has spent much of her life working in the Middle East, has been able to move matters forward, not by setting deadlines but rather by letting her Middle Eastern counterparts control the issue of time. She might start off a meeting by asking, "I want to respect your time, so how much time do you think we will need to conclude our business?"

Failing to accept other's values in a non-judgmental way will prevent you from truly understanding their U Perspective and using it to get what you want. You will end up wasting a great deal of time trying to get people to do things your way with little result. You are far better off using their U Perspective as a way to motivate people to work with you in order to achieve common goals. Remember, others may very well believe that your cultural perspective is the wrong one!

The French have a love/hate relationship with America. They resent what they consider the Americanization of their culture feeling that it usurps what is special about their country. At the same time they have a fascination with American culture. McDonald's epitomizes that paradox. It is such a symbol of American culture that in 1999 protesters bulldozed a half built McDonald's in Bove, France to protest the Americanization of French culture. The President of McDonald's France, Denis Hennequin, didn't simply dismiss this as an act of cultural extremists but recognized that the sentiment, if not the actions, reflected the U Perspective of many of his customers. While they loved the product they resented a further encroachment by America on French culture. Mr. Hennequin accepted that U Perspective and turned it to his advantage. After that incident he began a campaign to tell the French people more about McDonald's France and to blur the national lines about what kind of restaurant McDonald's France is. He emphasized that all the buns, meat and other ingredients used by McDonald's France are French (except for the cheddar cheese which comes from Netherlands) and that virtually all of their employees are French. As a result McDonald's France has prospered. There are now over 1,000 McDonald's in the country making France the third largest McDonald's market in Europe.

How individuals view contractual agreements is also a direct result of their culture. In the United States, which is very legally oriented, the agreement itself is sacrosanct. Americans seek to spell out agreements in detail attempting to cover every contingency that might arise. Parties are expected to strictly abide by the terms of the agreements they reach. Problems that arise are frequently resolved in court. In many cultures in Asia, Latin America and Europe, on the other hand, the party's relationship is paramount. The agreement is merely the starting point, subject to change as circumstances change. In China, for example, emphasis is placed on mutual cooperation and building relationships or "guanxi." The Chinese appreciate a sincere effort to work with them and will try to reciprocate whenever possible in the future. As a result, agreements are less detailed and less formal. When something isn't working well for one of the parties, the other is expected to adjust the terms of the agreement. In those cultures people are expected to work out problems between themselves. Courts are rarely used to enforce agreements.

Because relationships are frequently the key to successful business dealings in many parts of the world, a businessperson needs to make sure that he or she has involved everyone necessary to accomplish their objectives. In China a top down approach will not work. You need to proceed "kuai kuai," or block by block. It is not sufficient to deal only with the people at the top. You must make certain to build relationships at every level, an approach akin to the Buddhist practice of going to a temple and placing joss offering to the "little gods" as well as "big gods". In order to get things done you need to make sure you consider everyone from the CEO to the janitor and make sure their interests have all been taken into account. According to Ms. Chen Li Ping, Managing Director of The China Heping Construction Group (Far East) Pte. Ltd. and founder of the Innovative Corporation Pte. Ltd. an organization that promotes trade between Singapore and China, "while it might not be an easy job to establish trust with the Chinese, once it has been established, one can expect a strong and long lasting bond."

Borrowing from Edward Hall's classic work on cross-cultural dimensions, we can categorize how individuals perceive the world using four basic dimensions: relationship, time, communication style and formality. By understanding how a given culture thinks about each of these dimensions, one can gain insight into someone's U Perspectives. For example, some cultures, such as the United States, are deal focused. Those cultures have a short term orientation and expect any continuing relationship between the parties to be the byproduct of doing successful individual deals together. In contrast, businessmen and women in China, Japan and in many European and Latin American countries require a relationship before they will work with someone. These cultures have a longer term focus and expect that deals will be adjusted on an ongoing basis in ways that make doing business together mutually beneficial over the long term. Cultures that tend to be relationship driven also tend to be more collectivist in their orientation.

As discussed above, how time is viewed will range from the monochronic where punctuality is expected and timetables are adhered to strictly to the polychronic, where deadlines are fluid and nurturing relationships take precedence over completing your to-do list. Different cultures will fall in various places along that continuum.

Communication style also differs from culture to culture, frequently giving rise to misunderstandings. Cultures can either be high context or low context. In high context cultures, the meaning of what is being said is dependent on the context in which it is said. The listener is expected to figure out what is intended. Societies, such as Japan and Thailand where harmony, group consensus, and formality are favored in social interactions, tend to be high context in terms of how they communicate. In those cultures, yes doesn't necessarily mean, I agree. In Japan "Kai", which literally translates into English as "yes" usually means "I understand what you are saying" not "what you are saying is okay with me." The word "no" is rarely used in high context cultures. Often the same word can mean several different things allowing individuals to avoid conflict and not lose face. The Chinese also favor a high context style and according to Ms. Chen Li Ping, when dealing in China people need to "learn to read between the lines."

Americans, who favor a low context communication style, often misperceive high context communications and consider people who favor such a style to be devious. In cultures such as the United States, Germany and Switzerland, where a low context communication style is favored, there is an expectation that messages will be clear, concise and to the point. The speaker is expected to be direct and to ensure that the other person understands what is being said. Yes means yes not "go on" or "maybe." This communication style can give rise to outward conflict which is uncomfortable for individuals who are accustomed to a high context style of communication. Being direct can also be perceived as rude in certain cultures.

Hall's fourth dimension is personal space. This refers to how close you can stand near someone without making them feel uncomfortable. In Latin America, France, Italy, and the Middle East, for example, people do not expect a lot of personal space. You can get very close when speaking. The opposite is true in Germany, China, and Switzerland. While it is useful to be aware of these cultural preferences, they tell one very little about how to deal with someone from those countries beyond respecting their personal space.

The concept of formality would seem to be a more useful dimension to use, although to some extent it correlates with Hall's concept of personal space. Understanding how much formality a particular culture requires helps one better understand how people think and how best to work with them. Formality has to do with respect for authority, the need to follow etiquette and protocol, the ability of a single individual to make decisions and a person's willingness to take risks and to try new things. It also dictates how one should dress and behave. For example, according to Maria Sastre, generally in Latin America, "formalities are valued, and respect for their culture is important. Being informed about the local economy, political climate, position on issues and other public issues, is extremely important."

To be able to exert cross-cultural influence requires that you research the culture where you will be working. Be prepared for differences in how people view time, relationship, formality and communication. Most importantly, accept, without being judgmental, the differences in U Perspective that arise from differences in those cultural dimensions. Hire a skilled interpreter who can not only help you with the language, but serve as a cultural guide as well. Be patient. Bear in mind that whatever you do will take longer when you are doing it cross-culturally. If misunderstandings occur, and they will, slow down and try to find common ground. Avoid trying to impose your Me Perspective on those you are dealing with and you will be surprised at how much easier and more successful you will be doing business wherever you happen to find yourself.

Understanding how a particular culture views each of these dimensions will give you a cultural backdrop against which you can evaluate the U Perspective of the people with whom you are dealing. Be aware, however, that cultural stereotypes are just what their name implies – stereotypes. Not all Japanese avoid giving direct answers. Not all Germans are orderly. Not all Italians are expressive. Not all Thais are non-confrontational. Never forget that a person's U Perspective is individual to them. Age, as much as culture, plays a major role in how someone sees a given situation. Similarly professional training and corporate culture will also affect someone's U Perspective.

The mass media and the internet are creating a world culture or are, at least, greatly reducing cultural differences. Many young executives speak several languages, are well traveled and have studied or worked overseas. Veteran executives around the world are also more likely to have had assignments abroad and to have developed greater cultural sensitivity. Beware of over reliance on cultural stereotypes. As Ms. Chen Li Ping told me, "China is changing rapidly and so are the Chinese people, and hence never rely on yesterday's experiences and observations." Maria Sastre echoed a similar sentiment in noting that Latin American cultures are diverse and specific knowledge of the culture of a particular country is important if you intend to do business in that country.

While you need to understand the culture, you also need to treat each person you deal with as an individual. Even if you are primarily dealing with people over the telephone or by e-mail, there is no substitute for getting to know them. Developing personal relationships can be critical to business success. Try to meet people when you begin working with them. Use introductions from people they know and trust to help facilitate those relationships. Be careful when you communicate by e-mail, because in the absence of cultural context e-mails can easily be misunderstood. Most importantly, ask questions, listen and generally try to understand each individual's personal values and how he or she sees a particular situation - in short, their U Perspective.

Chapter 4

I am sure that nothing has such a decisive influence upon a man's course as his personal apperance.

Leo Tolstoy

Legitimacy: How You Look Affects How Others Behave

A popular television commercial starts with a cowboy speaking anxiously with the rodeo clown while he is sitting atop of a mean-looking bronco waiting to be let out of the chute into the rodeo ring. Between anxious breaths the cowboy thanks the clown and tells him that rodeo clowns can make the difference between riders walking away from a fall and incurring serious injuries. He expresses his gratitude to the clown who is beaming and graciously accepting as much praise as the cowboy wants to heap upon him. Then, as the stallion gives a final hefty buck before being released into the ring, the cowboy looks at the clown apprehensively and asks, "How long have you been a rodeo clown anyway?" The clown replies, "Me? I'm not a rodeo clown! I'm here with the birthday party in the third row!"

Your ability to influence others begins with their impression of the power or position that you hold. First impressions, how you look and how you carry yourself, form the foundation of how people view you. Creating the right image will enhance your ability to persuade.

People tend to defer to authority. Understanding that psychological imperative is critical to your ability to influence others. Creating an aura of authority around yourself will add credibility to the positions that you espouse. You can create the appearance of authority, or as we call it legitimacy, in a number of ways.

To discover the U Perspective of others requires determining what someone will do in a given situation because of their past history, experiences, feelings, and values. The research necessary to reveal what it will take to garner someone's support and gain their agreement will undoubtedly reveal a great deal about the likes, dislikes, personal values and biases of that person as well. This information can also be used to help you establish legitimacy with that person. Legitimacy is a very powerful tool and lies at the heart of the U Perspective. But you can only establish your legitimacy if what you use to announce your position and status are recognizable to the person you're trying to influence. Legitimacy is in the eyes of the beholder.

For some occupations the power of visual recognition in establishing legitimacy is essential. Police officers, judges and doctors, for example, all dress in a way that conveys instantly that they are functioning in a role that sets them apart from the rest of us and gives us an indication of how we are expected to react to their presence and their directives.

Other more subtle forms of legitimacy also establish credibility and rank. For example, in a medical environment doctors indicate their status as doctors by the way they dress – their white coats, name tags and the medical instruments they carry. Only by seeing a diploma, however, or by doing some research, can you distinguish one type of doctor from another, a GP from a cardiovascular surgeon, or a doctor that graduated from a top medical school from one who hails from a lesser known university. Experts make sure that we are aware of their status by putting these legitimizing tools on display in their offices.

Most of us don't have jobs that so readily lend themselves to legitimization. This is why so many individuals display diplomas, awards, and photos with luminaries in their offices as a way to signal their legitimacy to visitors. These signposts proclaim how powerful this individual is. In today's flattened organizations where casual dress may be the rule these displays are useful tools for those of us who seek to understand a person's U Perspective. We can use what we learn from what someone has on display in his or her office to establish our own legitimacy in their eyes.

Being able to establish instant legitimacy is one of the attributes that sets apart those that can effectively exert influence over others and those that are less successful at doing so. Because they have determined what is needed to create the legitimacy they seek and because they are conscious of how they are being viewed by others, they make the necessary adjustments to their appearance to fit the image that is expected of them.

You need to be proactive in establishing your own legitimacy. You cannot assume that people know what you do or what your credentials are. In my different roles as a trainer, public speaker, consultant, and executive coach, I do different things to establish my legitimacy. While I am who I am and my credentials don't change, the image I present and the credentials I need to emphasize may be different depending on the situation. When I train or speak my expertise and my ability to communicate my knowledge are paramount. My books, appearances on television and awards for teaching excellence establish my credentials and I need to find ways to convey that information to the intended audience. As a consultant or a coach my background as the head of human resources for several well known companies or my degree from Harvard may be more important. How I dress reinforces the image I need to present. You might think that a dark business suit would work for all of these roles, and it does, but other ways of dressing work better at certain times.

Let's say someone hears me speak for the first time at a public event sponsored by a local Chamber of Commerce. At that function I would be introduced as Lee Miller, Managing Director of Negotiation-Plus.com an Adjunct Professor of Management at Seton Hall Business School and the author of *UP: Influence Power and the U Perspective.* I'd probably be dressed in a serious dark colored business suit with a classic tie. After my speech, I'd sign books for those who wanted me to. Taken as a whole the image I would present would be that of a professional who is not only very knowledgeable about his subject but can present it in an entertaining and informative way.

Now let's assume that after hearing me speak a member of the audience asks about the possibility of me doing an onsite workshop for their company. I would arrange to meet with her at her office to go over what type of workshop is needed. For this meeting, I would probably also wear a suit, but I would try to dress the way people in her industry dress. If she were in insurance, accounting, law or banking I might wear one type of suit and tie whereas if she were in entertainment or retail I would probably wear a different type of suit and tie. I wouldn't need to spend a lot of time establishing who I am or demonstrating my credentials because she would already be aware of them from having heard me speak but I would need to connect with her as a potential client and be sure she knew that I understood her business. I could move quickly to try to determine what she needed and what her U Perspective was.

Had my legitimacy not been previously established, I'd have had to spend a good part of that first meeting convincing her not only that what I had to offer was valuable but that I was the best person to provide those services. I'd bring along a bio, some articles about what I do and maybe a copy of one of my books to help create my legitimacy. In fact, in the situation described above, I might still do that so she has something to give others in her company that she might need to influence.

Later, when the time came to do the training program, I would probably wear a serious business suit and tie because that is what the audience would be expecting. However, I would take off my jacket shortly after I was introduced to make the audience feel more comfortable with me and freer to ask questions. By virtue of my introduction by the woman who had invited me to speak, and by my being in the front of the room, my legitimacy with those in attendance is immediately established. My goal then is to connect with my audience so that the training becomes a give and take. I can reinforce my legitimacy throughout the day by what I do and the knowledge I impart to the audience.

My legitimacy in this instance is being bestowed on me by others. I can help that along by giving the person introducing me a written introduction that they can use. This makes their life easier and assures me that they will emphasize the aspects of my background and expertise that will most effectively provide me with legitimacy in the eyes of my audience. Throughout the process, I am not only aware of how I am being perceived by others but I also do whatever I can to help the process along by dressing and acting the part and reminding my listeners of the reasons that they want to hear what I have to say.

Many young professionals think that it's more important to project their own personal style rather than to conform to the expectations of others. That may be the case at a party where you are seeking to attract like-minded individuals, but as a real estate agent trying to close a deal or a businessperson seeking to gain the agreement of one's colleagues, personal style needs to take a back seat to the expectations of those you hope to influence.

A real estate agent that had just closed a $2.3 million deal told me the following story. A property had been on the market for over a year. It was a beautiful house situated on a fabulous piece of land with fantastic water views. The house should have sold quickly but it lingered on the market. The property was listed with the agency employing the grandson of the landowner and only he was allowed to show the property. Co-broker showings were prohibited. The grandson was young, inexperienced and not a particularly good salesperson; moreover, he was cocky, self-absorbed and overly impressed with the fact that his family owned the property. He dressed like a beach bum and wanted to be the center of attention in every situation. Because his grandmother would only give the listing to the agency if they agreed to employ her grandson, he was allowed to continue behaving in this manner despite his lack of success.

When the grandmother died, with the property still unsold, a family feud erupted and the property was placed in the hands of the probate court for disposal. The exclusive listing with the real estate agency that employed the grandson was terminated and the property was shown by numerous brokers via multiple listings. The property sold almost immediately for the full asking price. It goes without saying that the grandson was not the agent responsible for the sale. The difference between a buyer putting up the $2.3 million asking price in cash to buy the house and it sitting on the market unsold had nothing to do with the property itself but had everything to do with the appearance, attitude and approach of the salesperson.

Purchases of expensive homes and other luxury goods are made in part because of the mystique associated with what is being purchased. Our vision of what goes along with those items is fed on a daily basis by advertising and the media in general. A buyer imagines a lifestyle that goes along with the property. That is usually part of the U Perspective of the buyer and why the buyer is interested in what is being sold in the first place. If the image the broker presents is not consistent with what the property represents to a potential buyer, he or she may come to believe that the property is not what they are seeking. Successful real estate agents dress in a way that establishes their legitimacy. What they want their appearance to say is "I'm experienced and successful, I know what I'm doing and you can trust me to help you. I care about what you want." Each of us may have a slightly different picture in our mind of what that image is, and it clearly would look different in New York than in Kansas City. But the grandson's failure to present the expected image prevented him from making what was otherwise a relatively simple and straightforward sale.

Projecting the right image as a salesperson is especially tricky because every purchaser has a slightly different expectation of what a successful salesperson looks like. Even so, you need to pay close attention to the reaction you receive from others when you walk into a room and adjust your appearance until more often than not you get the reaction that you desire. Image helps to create or destroy legitimacy. How we look and how we carry ourselves are essential ingredients, but it's the perception of others that matters because they are the ones who confer legitimacy upon us. Not only do you need to establish what legitimacy looks like to those you seek to influence, but once you find the right look you still need to check in from time to time as your situation, and age, change.

Here's a story that I've heard Barbara tell our workshop participants over and over again about how she periodically fine tunes her look. From time to time, when Barbara notices that people are not reacting to her as she expects, she goes shopping. Barbara goes to an upscale department store dressed as she would for the situation she is concerned about. Once she gets there, she seeks out a salesperson in the women's department and explains her situation – that her look needs some changes. The salesperson will inquire about what aspect of her appearance Barbara wants to change. In reply, Barbara asks the salesperson to guess what she does for a living. Based on the answer, Barbara asks what items in her appearance led the salesperson to that conclusion. Then they go to work together to make the necessary changes. Barbara tries on different outfits and accessories and when she thinks "the look" is right, she approaches other shoppers in the store and asks them to guess what she does for a living. Eventually, the salesperson and Barbara zero in on what adjustments she needs to make.

Barbara tells me that she learned this trick when she changed jobs and she had to be sure others reacted to her the way she wanted them to in her new role – for example when she left a high powered government job and became a consultant. Both positions required her to look powerful and confident, but in her government job she wanted a tough, no-nonsense look whereas in her consulting role she wanted to be perceived as warmer and more open.

Age also plays a part in how a person is viewed. Age, when equated with experience, tends to confer legitimacy, giving one more options in terms of how to dress. When you have to worry less about creating an aura of authority because of your age or your title, you are freer to dress slightly more casually in ways that may encourage others to open up with you.

Making it easier for others to know how they are expected to react to you is an essential part of how one uses the U Perspective. It is always easier to influence others when you look and act the way they expect someone in your position to look and act. When you allow others to quickly understand your role, position, and power, they will react accordingly. When you send confusing messages by the way you dress or act, others may react to you in a way that later on they find embarrassing. Usually when you have embarrassed someone, they seek to avoid you. In that event, the best you can hope for is a more expensive and difficult deal reflecting the price of their embarrassment. To avoid such situations, always send clear messages about who you are. Dress and act in a way that is attuned to the needs of the situation and the audience, even if that isn't the way you would choose to present yourself in different circumstances. As I once advised my son, you don't have to wear your earring when you go on a job interview or when you go to work if doing so is going to turn off the interviewer or make you less effective at work.

How you dress does make a statement about who you are but people sometimes forget that they are in control of the statement they choose to make. You can choose to make different statements at different times. It is not disingenuous to do so. Rather it takes into account the U Perspective of the people you are seeking to influence in the same way that you do when you present an argument in the manner that you believe will be most persuasive to an audience in terms of their U perspective.

As will be further discussed in Chapter 5, when you Convince using experts who support your position or other people whose opinions are respected by those with whom you are dealing, you can enhance the legitimacy of your message. Adding the weight of experts provides tremendous psychological impact. Similarly, personal mastery of the subject matter that you are dealing with as well as a superior grasp of the details also creates legitimacy. No one likes to look foolish. So once you have demonstrated that you have superior knowledge and experience in a particular area, people will be more likely to accept your opinions without challenging them. Interestingly, demonstrating a real expertise in one area has the effect of giving you a general aura of legitimacy that carries over into other areas. Reminding a listener of your own status - your title, your authority or your degrees - also adds legitimacy to what you are saying.

Calling upon personal connections is another way to confer legitimacy on yourself. Again research is essential. If you know that the person you are seeking to influence went to the same school as someone else that you know, or that he or she belongs to the same club or organization as one of your friends, you can start a conversation letting that individual know who or what you have in common. Of course, you want to make sure that there is a positive relationship between the two so that the name dropping doesn't backfire; your stock will rise in proportion to the regard with which the person you are meeting holds your friend. Legitimacy is transferred from your friend to you – so choose the people you refer to wisely. Do your research and remember the age old expression "you only get one chance to make a good first impression." How you make that impression is up to you!

Part Two:
The 3 Cs Method Of Influencing Others

NegotiationPlus™
3 Cs Influencing Method

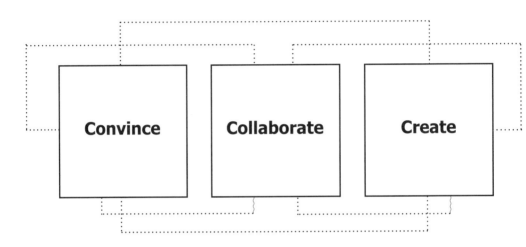

| Convince | Collaborate | Create |

- Anchoring
- Legitimacy
- Active Listening
- Purposeful Questioning
- Delivering the Message

- Developing Relationships
- Leveraging Relationships
- Determining Interests
- Problem-solving
- Taking Advantage of Value Differences

- Examining Assumptions
- Exploring Alternatives
- Trying Different Things
- Changing the People
- Creating New Paradigms

Chapter 5

I have no problem with authority. I just have a problem with people telling me what to do.

From the reality television show "Rollergirls"

Convince: Changing the Way Others Behave By Understanding What They See

Convince is often misunderstood as trying to persuade others that they should want what is being offered. That is why, until people embrace the concept of the U Perspective, they erroneously think that Convince is about getting someone to change their point of view. To the contrary, when we Convince, we demonstrate how what we are offering is something they already care about and want. Convince is not about showing someone that you are right and they are wrong, and that therefore they should do what you are proposing. Convince is about acknowledging that, at least from their vantage point, they are right and that therefore they should do what you are proposing. Once you accept that, you have taken the first step towards learning how to use the most powerful influencing tool on the planet - the U Perspective.

Convince is fact finding. Convince always starts with discovering the U Perspectives of those whom you wish to persuade. That knowledge will facilitate helping them to recognize that what you are seeking furthers their goals. By focusing on where you share common ground you reinforce the reasons why they are already inclined to do what you want them to do. Convince persuades by getting someone to recognize that which is familiar in what you are saying rather than to embrace something new. You are merely asking them to embrace values they already hold and showing them how what you are suggesting supports those values.

Trying to change someone's U Perspective is like trying to swim against the current. No matter how strong a swimmer you are, you will usually exhaust yourself before you reach your destination. Even a persuasive argument will fall on deaf ears if it goes against a person's core beliefs. That is because people tend to selectively focus only on those facts that support their preconceived ideas and because they interpret what they focus on through the prism of their prior experiences and the values they hold dear. In other words, they see what they want to see and believe what they want to believe.

In one experiment that illustrates this phenomenon, subjects were asked to evaluate the intelligence of a student they knew by reviewing information provided to them on a series of cards. The subjects were told to review one card at a time and to stop as soon as they reached a conclusion. Even though the information on each card was extremely damaging, when the subjects liked the student that they were evaluating, they continued to turn over one card after another, hoping to find something that would allow them to reach a favorable conclusion. On the other hand, when the subjects disliked the student they were evaluating, they turned over a few cards and quickly confirmed the conclusion they were already predisposed to reach.

The more you want to believe something the more you are willing to disregard facts that would contradict what you are predisposed to believe. According to *The Science of Sherlock Holmes* by E. J. Wagner, in 1866 Lady Tichborne of England, whose son had disappeared at sea 12 years earlier, was contacted by someone claiming to be her son Roger in response to an ad she had placed seeking information about her son's whereabouts. Despite the fact that this individual was taller than Roger, had brown eyes while her son's were blue, had a birthmark that her son did not have, did not have the tattoo her son got when he went off to sea and bore almost no resemblance to the son she remembered, she accepted this gentleman, later convicted of fraud, as her long lost son and gave him a £1,000 annual stipend. While grieving mothers might be forgiven for letting hope trump reason, people routinely ignore facts that contradict what they want to believe. For example, on a airplane recently the woman sitting next to me, a well educated accountant, described how her teenage son was vehemently opposed to using animals for medical research, but having grown up hunting with his dad, saw no contradiction in killing animals when he went hunting and opposing, as cruel, the use of animals for medical research.

If someone wants something they will find reasons
why they should have it. Moreover, how people value
things is not only subjective but can be influenced by
what others do. Because people hear what they want
to hear, persuasion requires that your arguments be
consistent with their U Perspective. People instinctively distrust what others tell them, especially if
they don't already have an established relationship
with the speaker. However, if you are merely con-
firming what someone already believes or appealing
to what they already care about, then they accept
what you are saying without questioning it.

When Lisa Caputo, now President of Citigroup's
Women and Co., was Press Secretary for First Lady
Hillary Rodham Clinton, she appealed to the values of the journalists covering the White House to
convince them to respect Chelsea Clinton's privacy.
In early 1993, for example, Mike Myers did a skit
on Saturday Night Live making fun of Chelsea who
was only thirteen at the time. Lisa contacted NBC,
but rather than trying to threaten or bully them, she
appealed to their U Perspective as parents, "Chelsea
is just a kid. She did not run for office. She deserved
as normal a childhood as possible under the circumstances. That is what you would want for your children, wouldn't you?" Although this issue arose periodically throughout the Clinton Presidency, by and
large, this sort of appeal to their values as parents
and as decent human beings worked with the members of the press. As to Mike Myers, he sent a letter
apologizing to the Clintons and NBC basically left
Chelsea alone over the next eight years.

Intellectually people may recognize that there may
be another way of seeing a situation other than the

way they see it. However, when all is said and done, down deep we always think ours is the right way. If we didn't believe that we would behave different- ly. If we haven't changed already it is because we have not been persuaded that it is in our interests to change. Rather than fight that human instinct, Convince embraces it.

Similarly, value tends to be subjective. What some- thing is worth depends on to whom it is offered and under what circumstances. People often want what others want, regardless of any inherent value an item may have. Status and social acceptance depend on what others value. Through marketing, businesses create brands that are status symbols for which con- sumers are willing to pay a premium, beyond what they would normally pay for goods of equal quality but which lack a status label. A shirt with a polo player or a crocodile logo costs more than a virtu- ally identical shirt without that symbol. Companies seek celebrity endorsers for their products to add ca- chet and enhance their value.

Convince seeks to highlight the connection between what you want and what the person you wish to influence already cares about. Integral to this ap- proach is an acknowledgement of the importance that emotions play in how people behave. Rather than seeking to defuse or deny those emotions, we accept them and utilize them to further our objec- tives. It is not necessary to get someone to change their U Perspective. In fact, we are doing exactly the opposite when we Convince. We are focusing people on those aspects of their own U Perspectives that are consistent with what we are seeking.

ANCHORING

Anchoring is a Convince tool used to impact how people view what you are proposing. Since value tends to be both relative and subjective, individuals typically determine value by looking for an anchor and then making adjustments relative to that point of comparison. Thus, where you begin the discussion often determines where it will end. Whether a discussion involves price, timing, or what you will do for someone, you can impact how they evaluate what you are proposing by the way you present it.

Let's consider how the anchoring concept applies in the context of determining the salary an employer decides to offer a job candidate. Ordinarily an individual's current compensation is used as the starting point, or anchor, in determining what is offered to a prospective new hire. Recruiters usually try to offer an amount that, based on an individual's current compensation, would be sufficient to motivate that person to change jobs. Even when a prospective employer recognizes that someone is grossly underpaid they will still use that individual's current salary as their starting point and make adjustments from that to take into consideration the low level of the individual's current compensation. Therefore the offer might be increased slightly but will still likely be below the prevailing market rate. If the employer did not know what the candidate was currently earning, however, they would have to look to the market in determining what to offer the candidate. If a candidate has another job offer, however, that becomes the anchor. In that instance the candidate's current salary becomes irrelevant, with the competing offer serving as the anchor in determining what salary to offer.

Empirical research supports the powerful effect anchoring can have on how people process information. Participants in one study were given a random number and then asked whether the number of African countries that were members of the United Nations was greater or less than that number. Then they were asked to estimate the percentage of U.N. members that were African. Even though the participants knew the number they had been given was chosen randomly, it still had a substantial impact on the estimates they gave. For example, the median estimate from participants who were given the number 10 was 25% as compared to 45% for those given the number 65. Even paying the participants based on the accuracy of their estimates did not change the impact of the anchoring effect.

Anchoring can be used not only to influence how financial issues, such as cost or salary, are resolved but also for a host of other issues as well. For example, what you initially ask for can also effect what someone is willing to do in terms of agreeing on a deadline. Thus, if you need something soon how you anchor your initial request will have a substantial impact on how quickly you actually get it.

When value cannot be easily determined, anchors play an even greater role in how we evaluate a proposal. Thus, normally the more you ask for, the more you will end up getting. There are exceptions to that rule. When you ask for something substantially beyond what would be considered reasonable, it has an inhibiting effect on any further discussion. Often the other party will simply walk away and refuse to discuss the matter any further.

Even though anchors need to be reasonable, in most situations there are many possible anchors one can choose from. Therefore you can select from among those choices the anchor that is most advantageous to you as long as you can justify what you are proposing. For example, when you are purchasing a home in a weak housing market, you might choose to anchor your offer based on the lowest price paid for a comparable house in the area and then lower that by a certain percentage to reflect the softening market. Or when you are assigned a project you could propose staffing the project with more individuals than had been assigned to previous projects of similar scope based on a desire to complete it more quickly.

Managing people's expectations is a form of anchoring and it is an important Convince tool. If expectations are too high, no matter what you propose it will not be enough. Individuals evaluate what you are proposing based on what they are expecting to hear. If what you are suggesting is better than what they were expecting they will react positively. If it is worse they will be unhappy. That is the case regardless of any objective measure of the value of what you are offering. Accordingly it is useful to try to lower expectations when you actually put forth a proposal.

Politicians routinely try to lower the expectations for their performance before a debate by having their people talk up how great a debater their opponent is. That way if they do well they will look even better by comparison and if their performance is poor it will be what was expected, but no worse.

Expectations can be set by how you construct your message and by the way you deliver it. Donna Lagani, Publishing Director for Cosmopolitan and Cos-moGirl, recommends that on key issues you set the expectations upfront. She calls this "using bullet-proof statements." For instance, she might say at the beginning of a discussion with a potential new advertiser, "We will work with you but there are certain things we won't do. We won't give away free advertising space to leverage additional business." That takes the issue off the table, once and for all.

You can also lower expectations by not giving in too quickly. The harder it is to gain a concession the more people will value it. For instance, a colleague of mine recently received a raise. It wasn't much. Ordinarily she would have been insulted by such a paltry increase. But, because her company was in bankruptcy and it was already long past the time when raises had been given in previous years, she wasn't expecting any raise at all. As a result she was happy with what she received.

Similarly how you frame the problem you are seeking to resolve often predetermines the outcome of a discussion. There is a television commercial selling gold coins that asks which you would rather have, one thousand dollars in gold or one thousand dollars in cash, if you were required to hold each for at least five years. The answer to the question, when it is framed that way, is of course the gold. The value of the dollar will likely erode because of inflation while gold has a chance of appreciating. Viewed in that light, buying gold would seem to make a lot of sense. Having lead the listener to that realization, the advertiser not only hopes that you will rush right out and buy gold, but that you will buy it from them. However, your choices are not limited to buying gold or keeping your cash under the mattress. You can buy gold, real estate, stocks, bonds or a myriad of other investments. Looking at the available choices in that light, buying gold may not seem like such a good idea after all.

Convince is always a dialogue, never a monologue. If you listen, people will tell you what they need in order to be persuaded. Listening is critical to understanding someone's U Perspective. That is why the active listening techniques discussed in Chapter 2 are such important Convince tools. In fact, sometimes a person's U Perspective is simply the need to be heard. As a human resources executive as well as a father, I have learned that people often think they are being ignored. We all have a need to be heard. It validates us. It is at the heart of any relationship, whether professional or personal. Many times, all someone really wants is for you to listen to them and acknowledge their point of view. If that is their U Perspective, letting them know that you have heard them and understand how they see the situation may be the first step toward gaining their cooperation. Sometimes that is all you need to do in order to get what you want.

As the head of human resources at several companies, I have had the difficult and delicate task of firing people. When that occurs, each side comes to the situation with very different U Perspectives. Ordinarily, in my position I would have reviewed and approved the decision to fire someone and would therefore approach the situation believing that the action being taken was appropriate. My goals when I met with the employee would be to have the individual feel that he or she was treated fairly and to have him or her exit quietly, without any litigation. Employees, on the other hand, often do not believe that they deserve to be fired. They want to be treated with respect and to receive a fair severance package. For many people, however, the most important thing is that they be allowed to have their say. They want to tell their side of the story. If you don't allow them to do that, no matter what else you do for them, they will feel that they have not been treated fairly. You have to understand their U Perspective and acknowledge those feelings.

Similarly, when you communicate with your children you need to listen to them and to acknowledge their feelings. Many times just making an effort to understand their U Perspective - how they see things - is enough to get them to go along with what you want them to do, even if they disagree with you. Showing respect for them and for their point of view is often more important to them than what they are asking for. In order for someone to be open to listening to you, they need to feel that you are listening to them. Influencing others always begins with listening to them.

PURPOSEFUL QUESTIONING

Asking purposeful questions is important in determining and subsequently taking advantage of someone's U Perspective. Different types of questions are used for different purposes. The two primary reasons for asking questions are to gather information or to use someone's U Perspective to advance your position. The best way to ask a question depends on what you seek to accomplish.

If your goal is to obtain information ask open-ended questions. Open-ended questions are those that can not be answered with a yes or a no. These are questions that usually begin with who, what, where, when, why or how. Open-ended questions allow you to learn what someone is thinking. Their unstructured nature enables you to find out what is really at issue and how the situation might be resolved to everyone's satisfaction. Open-ended questions like: "Tell me how you reached that conclusion" can also give you an insight into how another person thinks and what their U Perspective is.

Whether you are successful in obtaining the information you seek often depends on how you ask a question. Donna Moneta, a former journalist and now a private investigator for Investigative Consultants LLC, describes some of the ways that she gets people to provide information. She seeks to understand the U Perspective of the people she is speaking with and uses that to garner their assistance. If approached in the right way most people want to be helpful. Being empathetic takes advantage of people's desire to help. Statements like, "I understand why you might be hesitant about sharing that but it would really help if you did," work well for her and generally result in people providing her with the information she needs. Donna also finds that asking questions confidently and matter-of-factly encourages people to respond even where sensitive information is involved. As we will discuss later in this chapter, asking questions in that way lends legitimacy both to her and to her questions making it more likely that people will respond.

Acting as if you don't understand something is another way to gather information. If you ask lots of questions and look like you need assistance most people are naturally inclined to want to lend a hand. In the past, I have referred to this as the "Columbo" technique, after the bumbling television detective who, by acting as if he did not understand anything, was always able to get the criminal to tell him what he needed to find out in order to crack the case. When you ask for people's help their defenses come down and they often unintentionally provide you with useful information. They will also likely reveal a lot about their own U Perspective. Limit how you use this approach to situations where the person you are dealing with would be expected to be more knowledgeable than you are. Otherwise it may undermine your credibility. For the same reason, you do not want to overuse this technique.

Often the most useful question you can ask is why. Asking why works particularly well when you are responding to a statement such as: "We can't do that." or "That would be contrary to our policy." When you ask "Why can't you agree to that?" or "Why do you have that policy?" it calls for a reasoned response. Once someone has committed to a reason for their position acting consistently with the proffered reason becomes a part of their U Perspective. You can then make a case that the reason they have provided is not applicable in this instance. Alternatively, you have an opportunity to satisfy the objections that have been raised.

Another way to get someone to provide you with information is to use a variation on the reflecting back technique described in Chapter 2. Simply repeat what has just been said in question form. If someone takes an unreasonable position, you can use this reflecting back technique to get them to rethink their stated position by taking advantage of the fact that people universally want to be viewed as reasonable. When their own words make them look foolish, most people are quick to change their position. For example, if you were talking to a company with a New York based sales force about distributing your product in the Northeast and they sought an exclusive right to distribute your products throughout the United States, you might use this technique to respond as follows:

Distributor: We want an exclusive right to distribute your product throughout the United States.

You: But you have no sales network outside the Northeast.

Distributor: We think we will be able to build one over the next few years.

You: You think you will be able to build one over the next few years?

Simply reflecting someone's own words back to them when they are taking a position that is not reasonable can be extremely persuasive.

Similarly when someone makes unqualified statements such as, "We never do that." A simple "Never?" will force them to either confirm that this is in fact the case or more likely cause them to retreat to something like, "except in very unusual circumstances." For example, you might use this technique if you are discussing relocation in connection with a job offer.

Employer: Relocation is always governed by

	the terms of our relocation policy.
You:	Regardless of the circumstances?
Employer:	Well, except in very unusual circumstances.

Once you have gotten that admission you are on your way to getting what you are asking for. Now you know that you need to stress that yours are unusual circumstances that require an exception to the normal policy. The U Perspective of most recruiters and hiring managers includes a desire to be fair and to make the person they are recruiting feel wanted. Once someone has conceded that they sometimes go beyond their normal relocation policy, it becomes much harder to deny your request consistent with that U Perspective. Doing so would be tantamount to saying that you don't deserve to be granted treatment similar to what has been afforded to others in the past.

Finally if you find yourself at an impasse in your deliberations, you can always ask someone what they would do if they were in your position. This harnesses their U Perspective to your advantage and can sometimes completely change the direction the discussions. It forces the other person to try to come up with a solution to the problem, rather than trying to convince you that there is no problem. In doing so they may offer a solution that would be acceptable to you or could be made to be with some slight modification

Cathy Harbin is a former professional golfer and General Manager of the two golf courses at the World Golf Village, the home to the Golf Hall of Fame. Cathy uses purposeful questions to refocus someone's U Perspective. Using questions she also creates legitimacy based on her superior experience and knowledge. She frequently uses this technique when she is meeting for the first time with men that want to hold tournaments at the courses that she manages. For example, someone might come in all blustery and say to her, "I want to hold a tournament and pay $50 per person in green's fees, be able to bring donated beverages and be given a twenty percent discount on food and merchandise." She will repeat what they just said to her, "You want to pay $50 per person in green's fees, to be able to bring donated beverages and be given a twenty percent discount on the price of food and merchandise." She will ask, "Do you really think that is fair?" Then she will wait for a response. That normally results in the prospective customer revealing his U Perspective and telling her what he really wants. For instance, he might reply, "Well what I really need is a $50 green's fee" or "I need to keep the total cost of the event under $10,000." Once she has that information, it's relatively easy to work out an arrangement that satisfies everyone.

Cathy also uses questions to establish her legitimacy when a good golfer, usually a man, who has never run a tournament, comes in to talk about running a tournament for his company or for a charitable organization. He thinks he knows all about tournaments because he has played in a few. He may even believe he knows more about running one than Cathy because she is a woman. Now Cathy could tell him when he asks for a $35 green's fee that he doesn't have a clue and she is sometimes tempted to do that. If she did, however, she probably wouldn't get his business. So she tactfully educates him by asking purposeful questions. The conversation might go something like this:

> Golfer: At the last tournament I played in they charged a $35 green's fee.
>
> Cathy: Where was that tournament held?
>
> Golfer: At Joe's Fleabag Motel and Golf Emporium.
>
> Cathy: Is that a lot like our courses?
>
> Golfer: Not exactly.
>
> Cathy: I see. Well have you run tournaments before?
>
> Golfer: Not really, but my club runs one and I was on the committee last year.
>
> Cathy: OK. What type of format do you want to use?
>
> Golfer: I don't know. What would you suggest?
>
> Cathy: Well, if most of the golfers are not in your league maybe you should go with a scramble and play best ball. What type of contests do you want to have?
>
> Golfer: I hadn't thought about that? How about closest to the pin? How many should we have? What do you suggest?
>
> Cathy: You might also want a longest drive contest. Do you want the beverage cart charged to the master account or do you want the golfers to pay as they go?
>
> Golfer: I don't know. What do other companies do?

Soon the golfer realizes that he doesn't know as much about running tournaments as he thought. At the same time, Cathy makes certain that he understands that her goal is to help make sure the event is a huge success - which, after all, is usually his U Perspective. By the time they get down to discussing the price and the other details of the event, the conversation has become more of a collaboration about how to design a great event and still stay within the organization's budget, rather than a negotiation over price.

STRUCTURING YOUR MESSAGE

If you have done a good job of listening and asked the right questions, you will have laid the groundwork to persuasively deliver your message. Convince is not just about the substance of your message though; it is also about the messenger and how the message is presented. Put differently, your ability to Convince someone depends not only on what you say and how it is presented (content and structure), but also how you say it (tone), and the authority with which it is presented (legitimacy of the message and the person delivering it.) While the content of your message is important, research has shown that how your message is delivered can be as important as the actual message itself. Let's consider each of these items separately.

Construct your message to support the U Perspectives of the people you seek to influence.
Always craft your message with the U Perspective of the person you are seeking to influence in mind. You persuade in terms of what people care about.

When you focus on what people already care about, very little persuasion is actually necessary because they are predisposed to agree with you. In addition to showing them how what you are proposing satisfies their U Perspective, structure your discussions in the manner that will be most effective with your intended audience. Think about constructing your message the way your ninth grade English teacher taught you to write essays in high school – start with a theme, use arguments in support of that theme, add facts to buttress your arguments and structure everything to convincingly present it all.

Create a theme that reflects the audience's U perspective. Once you have marshaled your facts and determined what the best arguments are in terms of the U Perspective of the people you are seeking to influence, you need to pull them together into a theme. A theme serves as the organizing principle around which to structure your discussions. Tailor the theme to the people you are trying to persuade. This can be done in one of two ways. First, you can appeal to the individual's self interest - one aspect of people's U Perspective. This is the type of appeal that we normally think of when we think about sales or negotiating. This is what collaborating is all about. An appeal of this type is based on what the other party wants or needs. It focuses on the other party's interests. For example, your appeal could be, "If you give me a raise, you will have my undying loyalty, hard work and someone that can help you obtain that promotion you are hoping for." Those same arguments also could be presented in the negative, "If you don't give me that raise I will leave, thereby depriving you of a loyal, hardworking employee that you really need in order to get the promotion you want." But arguments are generally more powerful when phrased positively. It is far more compelling to be for something than against something. That is why individuals who oppose abortion describe themselves as "pro-life" rather than "anti-abortion."

The second type of theme is designed to appeal to values. Under certain circumstances you may want to appeal to a sense of fairness or focus on how your proposal benefits others (i.e. a charity). If you are going to appeal to someone's values, you have to recognize what is important to them. That is why it is important to find out everything you can about the people you want to influence so that you will truly understand their U Perspective and be better able to exploit it to move them in the direction you would like. Appeals to certain values can be particularly effective with family members and friends. Appealing to their generosity and a desire to help will often have the desired impact.

Themes are particularly important if you are dealing with someone representing an organization, whether it is a corporation, the government or even the PTA. In such situations, you not only have to satisfy the U Perspective of the person you are speaking with, but that person then has to persuade the members of their organization to accept what has been agreed upon. My early experience as a labor negotiator taught me the value of creating themes that reinforce your audience's U Perspective. Themes should be simple and ring true to the intended audience. For example, during one negotiation when I was working for Macy's in the 1980's the theme we chose was competitiveness, always a good theme if one is trying to cut costs. We argued the need to become more efficient in the face of non-union competitors. We highlighted the benefits to the union of our becoming more competitive - focusing on the U Perspective of their members - preservation of jobs and salary increases for current members. To buttress this theme we pointed to all the unionized retailers who had gone out of business in the prior ten years. We justified every proposal in terms of how it would make us more competitive. In the end the union reluctantly agreed to many of our proposals and was able to sell them to its membership.

The need to use themes that are consistent with the U Perspective of those you are trying to influence applies to personal situations as well. G.G. Michelson, formerly the Senior Vice President of External Affairs for R. H. Macy & Co. and a member of the Board of Directors at General Electric, Quaker Oats, Goodyear, Federated Department Stores, Stanley Works and Chubb Corporation, also started her career as a labor negotiator. At a time when there were very few female labor negotiators, she was bargaining with union leaders like Ron Carey, who later became President of the International Teamsters Union, and Peter Brennan, who later became Secretary of the United States Department of Labor. However, the negotiation of which she was the proudest was convincing her father to let her go to law school.

At the time she graduated from college, very few women attended law school. Her father firmly believed that, while it was okay for a young woman to work, her goal should be getting married and having a family. That being the case, her attending law school didn't make a lot of sense to him. So she sought to Convince her father in terms consistent with his U Perspective - how he viewed marriage and family. She sought to persuade him that, since she had graduated from college at 19, she needed to have additional credentials to be able to find meaningful work even if only until she got married. She added that it was important to prepare oneself for a lifetime of useful work, even though it might be interrupted for a time while she was raising a family. A law degree would help. She succeeded in convincing her father because she never tried to change his view of the role of marriage and family. She never challenged his core values - how he saw the situation. Instead, she persuaded him that what she wanted was consistent with his U Perspective.

Consider what will motivate someone to want to do what you are proposing. Focus on what the people you are seeking to influence care about. For some that might be money. For others it might be status. For yet others it might be helping a worthy cause. Whatever their U Perspective is, you want to build your theme around it. Once you understand their motivation, then you can construct a message that not only satisfies those needs but also overcomes their objections.

Nancy Erica Smith, when she is trying to settle an employment dispute, always listens for the underlying subtext - the unstated obstacles to agreement. She tries to determine what the other side needs in order to save face. According to Nancy, many times what impedes a settlement is not money. The parties are generally able to realistically figure out what a case is worth. Often, however, the person who initially made the decision being challenged, usually a termination, has a say in whether or not to settle. This person may not even be directly involved in the settlement discussions, yet their U Perspective may result in their trying to prevent any settlement. In their mind, they equate settling with an admission that they did something wrong. In that situation, Nancy might use a theme that places the blame on someone else. For example, she might fault someone for withholding key information from the person who made the termination decision. This allows the decision-maker to settle the case without having to admit doing anything wrong.

Tailor your message to the intended audience. When trying to Convince someone, highlight the benefits to the other party of what you are suggesting and focus on how it supports their values. Whether you are negotiating a multi-million dollar movie deal or simply deciding on what movie to see with a friend, keep coming back to why what you are suggesting is a good idea for them in terms of what they care about. Describe the benefits in different ways. Repetition reinforces your message. There is a saying in advertising, "Tell them what you are going to say. Say it. Then tell them what you just said." But be careful. Repetition can easily be overdone and start to detract from your message. So another way of bringing home your message is to make sure everything relates back to a theme designed with U Perspectives of your audience in mind.

Not only do you need to make certain that the content of your message is consistent with the U Perspectives of your audience but you also need to present that message in terms they will relate to. Consider how the person you are seeking to influence likes to process information. If someone is primarily interested in the big picture emphasize the results that will flow from what you are proposing. If someone is a strategic thinker explain why you believe the proposal will deliver the desired results. For someone who is detail oriented, particularly for people who might be described as micromanagers, go over what will occur in great detail.

Speak to your audience in their language. You should present information in familiar ways. If your audience consists of business people a Power-Point presentation might be appropriate; you would also want to use phrases, like "bottom line," that the members of your audience would normally use. Similarly, when presenting to government officials you might want to use information that they have developed themselves and focus on the "policy implications" of what you are proposing.

The specific words you chose to describe something can also be important and need to reflect the U Perspective of the people you are dealing with. Lynn Newsome, a prominent divorce lawyer, was handling a case where the couple involved could not agree on anything. The husband was insisting on joint custody of the children. He was adamant on that point and wouldn't accept anything less. Lynn represented the wife who had been responsible for making all the decisions involving the children during the marriage. Her client was afraid that her husband would use joint custody rights to harass her. Based on the husband's behavior while they were working out the divorce settlement, she had legitimate reasons for concern. Lynn was able to resolve that issue by simply using language that reflected the husband's U Perspective. She proposed that the parties have joint custody but that her client, the mother, have sole decision making authority for most aspects of the children's lives. This satisfied the husband's U Perspective and avoided a costly custody battle.

Create legitimacy for your message. In Chapter 4 we discussed how you create legitimacy for yourself in order to enhance your ability to influence others. You can also create legitimacy for your message. The power of legitimacy derives from the fact that people are programmed to defer to authority. To the extent you can invoke authority to support what you want, people are more likely to accede to your wishes. Accordingly, you may choose to support your message by relying on experts or other people whose opinions are respected by the people with whom you are dealing. Adding the weight of experts provides tremendous psychological impact. Experts can be used to great effect in your personal as well as your business dealings.

For example, when Gina Doynow, the manager of College Credit Services for Citicorp, was decorating her apartment she thought a brown rug would go nicely in the living room. Her husband always hated brown. He would not even consider a brown rug. So she brought in their decorator, someone whose taste her husband respects. The decorator was able to get him to look at brown rugs. Today they have a beautiful brown rug in their living room that her husband loves. Similarly, when G.G Michelson was trying to convince her father to allow her to go to law school, she met with two of her father's friends who were lawyers. They informed her father they thought

G.G. would make a great lawyer. While there were other ways for her to persuade her father, having people that he respected support her had a psychological impact that far exceeded whatever specific point they made on her behalf. Reminding the listener of your own status - your title, your authority or your degrees - can also lend to the legitimacy to what you are saying.

You can add legitimacy to the terms of your offer when you selling or negotiating by presenting someone with a printed form contract or by relying on company policy to support your position, particularly if you can point to something in writing, like a policy manual. When you invoke policies or standard forms it gives the appearance that you are powerless to change your position. Like using an expert, basing your position on something authoritative provides the facade of objectivity. Therefore, it carries greater weight. When someone tells you, "That is the way it is always done," it is intended to have the same effect. While you can take advantage of this human tendency when you are seeking to influence others, keep in mind that just because an expert says something or because it is printed in a manual does not mean that you have to agree with what is being suggested. You can always bring in your own expert, print up your own forms, point to your own policies or simply disagree. You can respond to "This is the way it is always done" with "Well, we always do it this way." In short, you can use legitimacy to Convince but do not be intimidated when someone else seeks to invoke it.

Choose the proper tone for your message. The tone used to convey your message matters. Not only is what you say important, but so is the way you say it. If you doubt that, think about the words to the children's lullaby *Rock a Bye Baby*: "Rock a bye baby on the tree top, when the wind blows the cradle will rock. When the bough breaks the cradle will fall, and down will come baby, cradle and all." These are pretty gruesome words. Yet, because of the soothing tone of the lullaby, we sing it to our children to calm them and put them to sleep. No one pays any attention to the words. As Marshall McLuhan said, "The medium is the message." Tone is not only conveyed by the spoken word; your choice of words can convey tone, for instance, friendliness or anger. The tone you chose should be designed to convey the desired message in terms of what people expect in light of their U Perspective. As my daughter and I discovered in researching *A Woman's Guide to Successful Negotiating*, when a man takes a tough position he needs to use a tough tone or his audience will not believe he is serious but when a women takes a tough position she usually is more effective using a confident, quiet, firm tone.

Even if you are soft-spoken, it helps to be passionate about your point of view. One thing that Lisa Caputo learned from watching Hillary Clinton when she was her Press Secretary was the importance of believing in what you are saying. "Your passion can persuade others. It is always an invaluable trait to be passionate about your beliefs and what you are striving for. Your passion makes you more credible and somewhat easier." Cathleen Black, President of Hearst Magazines, put it this way: "If you are passionate about something you can sell an idea. If you are passionate it builds an inherent strength and confidence. All of us love to see real enthusiasm in the people around us. It is infectious. If you are enthusiastic you will probably get more." People can generally tell if you really believe in what you are saying. If you don't, it will be very hard to Convince anyone else to agree with you.

Pay attention to how your audience reacts to your message and adjust the message accordingly. Even with all the preparation in the world, we can never fully anticipate how our message will be received. As soon as someone other than yourself becomes involved you can no longer predict what will happen because, by definition, the other party has a different U Perspective. Your monologue becomes a dialogue. Military planners have a saying: "no plan survives contact with the enemy." You have to incorporate the other person into the process. Constantly reframe your message to incorporate input from the people you are dealing with to be sure you are taking into account their U Perspectives.

When we Convince we not only need to listen but also to react to what is said. We can respond in one of three ways: address the arguments being made directly to provide additional information or correct misunderstandings, modify our message to better satisfy the other person's U Perspective or grant concessions to enhance the real and/or perceived value of what is being offered. Normally we will do all three. Convince works best when you have taken the time and effort to discover someone's U Perspective. By couching your discussion in terms of what others deem important you do not have to persuade them of anything. You merely have to remind them that what you are proposing is something they have already decided that they want. You can affect how someone perceives the value of what you are offering using various Convince tools as long as you start off by offering them something that they already value. The power of the U Perspective is that it relies on what people not only already believe, but what they believe deeply.

Chapter 6

It is one of the most beautiful compensations of this life that no man can sincerely try to help another without helping himself.

Ralph Waldo Emerson

Collaborate: Using Relationships To Find Ways To Satisfy Everyone's Interests

If Kitty D'Alessio, the former President of Chanel, had to point to the one thing she did that was instrumental in her turning around the fortunes of the company, it would be hiring Karl Lagerfeld to design their line. By the time Kitty joined Chanel, Karl Lagerfeld had already become one of the hottest designers in the world. In addition to designing clothing for Chloe, he was designing furs for Fendi and was selling fragrances under his own label. He was also already earning more money than Chanel could possibly afford to pay him. But even though she had never met him she understood what she needed to do in order to hire him.

Kitty knew what would motivate him to accept a position with Chanel because she understood his

U Perspective. Lagerfeld had everything a young designer could want, except the challenge and the prestige of designing a couture line. Kitty knew that by offering him the opportunity to design their couture line, she was offering him something he wanted more than money — a chance to attain the status that he aspired to as a designer. To induce him to come to work for Chanel, despite their inability to pay him what he could earn elsewhere, she agreed to let him continue with his other businesses at the same time that he was designing couture and ready-to-wear for Chanel, something unheard of at that time for a designer at a major fashion house.

This is Collaborate at its best. Chanel needed a creative designer for their couture and ready-to-wear lines. Designing a French couture line afforded Lagerfield status he could not get in any other way. By allowing him to retain his other ventures, Chanel was able to hire him and still stay within their limited budget. The key to Kitty's reinvigorating the Chanel line by hiring Karl Lagerfield was her ability to determine his U Perspective and to design a solution that enabled him to obtain what he desired most at that moment. Knowing what she needed to do, she used Collaborate techniques to accommodate his needs at the same time satisfying Chanel's interests.

Collaborate is a problem solving process that entails four basic steps: developing a relationship, understanding the other party's interests and their U Perspective, identifying options and agreeing on a mutually acceptable solution from among those options.   Once you understand what the other party's interests are, and have explored all the possible solutions, you can determine which one most effectively meets everyone's needs. Using these Collaborate techniques where appropriate, along with your Convince and Create skills, will enable you to achieve the best possible results.

Collaborate enables you to exert influence by employing a rational, interest-based problem solving approach. It works best where the U Perspective of the people that you are seeking to influence is logic-based - for example when someone is focused on getting the best possible economic deal for himself or his organization. The goal when you Collaborate is to find a solution that maximizes what everyone gets or at least those things each person cares most about. Even when you use the Collaborate approach to find an optimum solution for everyone, you still need to use Convince techniques. It does little good for you to Collaborate and come up with an excellent result for everyone if the people you are working with feel that somehow you have taken advantage of them.

Collaborate uses consensus building to find the best overall solution for everyone, not simply the best solution for you. In finding a mutually beneficial solution it is helpful to be able to read the people involved, to figure out what is important to them and what motivates them. To do that you often have to be able to sense what is going on beneath the surface by listening under and hearing what is not being said. Frequently the best Collaborate solution is a unique one that wasn't initially presented by either side. Yet Collaborate solutions usually work well and last because they are arrived at by addressing the U Perspective directly, not only to maximize what everyone gets, but also to insure that each party gets what they care about most.

The key to successfully Collaborate is developing and maintaining relationships. Relationships facilitate collaboration. Once you develop a relationship with someone you both have a stake in reaching a good outcome, a solution that works well for everyone not only at the moment but in the future as well. Moreover, to Collaborate effectively people need to share information honestly and candidly. That requires a level of trust that can only come about when you have developed a relationship. Relationship encourages people to eschew short term advantages in favor of taking the longer term view.

To develop relationships it helps to genuinely like people because it is human nature to like those people who like us. Building a relationship with someone begins with understanding their U Perspective. Listen to what they have to say. Look for common interests. Be friendly. Take time to get to know someone; it takes time to develop a relationship. Most importantly, go out of your way to do things for the people with whom you want to have a relationship. Strong relationships develop not because of what you get out of the relationships, but because of what you put into them. Kitty Van Bortel described the essence of collaborating when she stated that the secret of her success in building one of the largest Subaru dealerships in the country "is helping others get what they want."

Collaborate does not concentrate on what each party says they want; instead it focuses on their actual interests. What is the difference between wants and interests? Wants are what someone asks for. Interests are why they are asking for it. By identifying each party's real interests you can not only find ways to satisfies everyone's interests but to maximize those interests as well. Every professor who teaches negotiating tells the story of the two oranges to illustrate the importance of determining each person's interest when you seek to Collaborate. Two sisters are fighting over the last orange in the refrigerator. Both say that they need (want) the orange. If all we know is what they each want, one of them will be disappointed or perhaps they will each have to settle for half an orange. If we determine their interests, why they want the orange, then we may find a way to satisfy both their interests. In this case, one sister needs the orange rinds to bake an orange bunt cake and the other needs the pulp to make orange juice. Once the sisters know why each needs the orange, they can divide the orange in a way that allows them both to get 100% of what they need, rather than simply dividing the orange in half as most people would if they wanted to be fair but hadn't learned how to Collaborate.

Collaborate is problem solving. It is an iterative process that requires being able to keep everyone's interests in mind while trying to come up with a solution that meets all of their needs. Nancy Erica Smith, a well known New Jersey employment lawyer, describes this as multi-tasking. In her words, when you Collaborate "You are not going in to win but to find common ground. You are trying to meet many people's needs."

In their seminal work *Getting to Yes: Negotiating Agreement Without Giving In* Fisher, Ury and Patton describe a method for engaging in negotiations which they call principled negotiations. This is a form of collaborating. The Collaborate principles apply not only to negotiating but can be applied to any situation where you are seeking to influence someone. The goal is to be able to get what you want at the same time allowing others to do the same - in other words to find the best possible solution that that satisfies everyone. Over the years I have drawn heavily on *Getting to Yes* in developing my ideas about collaborating and am greatly indebted to the authors for their pioneering work.

Collaborate only really works if the other party wants to collaborate. You can sometimes create a situation where someone who is not initially inclined to collaborate with you chooses to do so. That is not always possible though. Collaboration is based on trust. It calls for open and honest communications which can only occur where a relationship exists. Otherwise the temptation to gain an immediate advantage by manipulating the process outweighs the benefits of working toward a mutually beneficial solution. If you believe that you can get anyone to Collaborate with you if you just approach them properly, try collaborating with a used car salesman. Nonetheless, understanding the salesperson's U Perspective and dealing with him or her in a way that satisfies those interests will allow you to get the best possible deal when you are buying a car.

Terrie Williams, President of The Terrie Williams Agency, a public relations firm that has represented Eddie Murphy, Miles Davis, Dave Winfield, Janet Jackson and Johnnie Cochran, among others, shares my belief that relationships are the cornerstone to success. According to Terrie, "To the extent you can develop a rapport with the person ... you can get almost anything. Any rule can be bent, broken or cease to exist if you have the right relationship. People do business with you because they like and respect you."

People have lots of choices in life about who they hire, who their friends are and who they do business with. Most people prefer to be around people they like. People will do business with you because they like you and enjoy working with you even though others may be equally or better qualified. Consistent with that U Perspective, when someone likes you they look for reasons to do business with you rather than reasons why they can't. It's also harder for people to say no to you if they like you.

Jeanette Chang, International Publishing Director at Hearst Magazine International, credits her success to the relationships she has developed. She puts that philosophy into practice on a daily basis. Almost all her business associates have become her friends over the years. To be able to develop relationships and to make the most of them it helps to become a more interesting person. One way she suggests doing that is to develop a hobby outside of your work. Hers is Asian art. The more interesting you are the more people will want to spend time around you. That will make it easier to develop relationships which, in turn, will make it easier to influence others.

It is always better to develop relationships before you actually need to influence someone. Although people may be suspicious if you attempt to do so shortly before you need something from them, even then, if your efforts to build a relationship are sincere, those efforts are likely to bear fruit. If you haven't been able to develop a relationship with someone ahead of time, it is not too late to try to do so when you first start to deal with them. Carole Cooper, one of the owners of the N. S. Bienstock Agency, is a successful agent representing writers, producers and television personalities. Her clients include Bill O'Reilly, Jack Ford and Soledad O'Brien. Before she enters into negotiations on behalf of one of her clients with someone she doesn't know she begins by trying to connect with that person as a person. Her preparation includes finding out about them personally - their interests, what their ratings are, industry gossip they might be interested in, etc. When she first meet them she talks about the pictures in their office, about their family, about the view, whatever she can do to find common ground.

Terrie Williams does the same thing. She gets together with someone in a relaxed atmosphere, for dinner or drinks, and tries to find out what they are all about. She seeks to understand their U Perspective. Her partner calls this opening a person's significance. "If you can zero in on what matters most to that person, you will better understand how to appeal to them," Terrie says. The more you can develop that relationship, the more successful you will be interacting with them.

Even when you are not able to get what you want immediately you can still use the opportunity to develop a relationship. Donna Lagani, Publishing Director for Cosmopolitan and CosmoGirl magazines, describes a situation where she was trying to sell advertising to a cosmetic company. They had just put in a new management team and did not have any money available at the time for advertising. Nonetheless, she met with them and listened to their concerns. She sought to determine their U Perspective. One of their major problems was attracting, and keeping, good beauty advisors to sell their lines in the stores. So Donna offered to hold a contest for their beauty advisors and to feature the winners in Cosmopolitan. Even though the company was not purchasing any advertising at that moment, Donna was willing to help them in order to develop a relationship. By running those contests, her magazine was able to stay in touch with the company's marketing people at a time when they were not meeting with any other magazines. Eventually when they began to advertise again, she was in an excellent position to garner a large share of that advertising due to the relationship she had previously built with their marketing department.

Sometimes just keeping everyone talking, and preventing them from drawing lines in the sand, will allow a sufficient relationship to develop so that the parties can Collaborate. An investment banker I know described a merger deal she was working on where price was the major stumbling block in putting the deal together. She was able, however, to keep the two sides in the room talking and resolving other issues. The more time the two management teams spent together the more they realized everything they had in common and how much the deal made sense. By the time it came to discussing price the parties had developed such an excellent working relationship that the price became less of a stumbling block. As a result, they were able to reach an agreement that proved to be advantageous to everyone.

Relationships you have already established can also be used to help facilitate collaboration with others. It often helps in forming a relationship to have mutual friends or acquaintances. That is why when we first meet someone we will typically mention individuals that we think the other person might know. Before Kitty D'Alessio ever contacted Karl Lagerfield she asked a mutual friend Grace Mirabella, then the Editor of Vogue, to call him. Kitty used that connection to create an instant relationship that she could immediately draw upon when she met with Karl.

Letting someone know that you have mutual friends exerts a powerful influence on them as well. Even if they will not have any further dealings with you, they are less likely to seek a short term advantage at your expense once they realize that you will be talking about them with mutual friends at some future date.

Opportunities to use your relationships to influence others frequently exist if you know how to take advantage of them. Susan Medalie, the former Executive Director of The Women's Campaign Fund, considers one of her greatest assets to be her talent for figuring out connections, who she knows that might be able to help. Often when you need something, the most important thing you can do is to determine who the right person is to ask.

When Susan was Deputy Director of The United States Holocaust Council she arranged to hold a "Day of Remembrance Dinner" in the Rotunda at the Smithsonian. This is a very elegant setting for an event and very difficult to get permission to use. One of the prominent features in the Rotunda is a huge pendulum that swings back and forth twenty four hours a day, seven days a week, which she feared might cause some people to get motion sickness while eating dinner. She recognized that it would be extremely difficult, if not impossible, for her to convince the people running the Smithsonian to stop the pendulum for any reason, let alone so she could hold a fundraising dinner. So she called Congressman Sidney Yates a strong supporter of the Holocaust Council. Through his committee assignments in Congress he had significant influence over the Smithsonian's appropriations. A request from him was all she needed to get the Smithsonian to stop the pendulum while dinner was being served. Sometimes the critical question when you are seeking to exert influence is who should be asking whom and how are they going to ask? Understanding the U Perspective of the people involved will help you come up with the right answer.

Little things can make a big difference in developing relationships. When Jeanette Chang goes to visit someone, for instance a designer who might want to advertise in one of her magazines, she reads up on fashion trends in her area. She looks at local newspapers. She tries to find out as much as she can about the company and the designer personally. She takes advantage of their U Perspective by bringing them an appropriate gift, based on what is going on in their lives at the moment. Jeanette recognizes that developing a relationship requires work. For her it has been worth the effort, in terms of being successful in all aspects of her life.

Collaborate requires understanding the nature of the other party's interests. When we Convince we seek to use someone's U Perspective to help them recognize that what we want them to do is something they already want to do. We start with our proposed solution and seek to move the other party toward our position by constantly readjusting our arguments and proposals to align them with the other person's U Perspective. Convince by its very nature is subjective. When you Collaborate, however, the focus is on the objective interests of the other person. While interests are always filtered through people's U Perspectives, to the extent you can keep everyone focused unemotionally on their objective interests, together you can work out a way to maximize what everyone gets.

For example, let's assume you own a piece of land on which you would like to build a vacation home. The property has a beautiful view of the lake. However, there is a piece of undeveloped land between your property and the water. Because you fear that the owner may develop the property and obstruct your view you want to purchase the land. Your neighbor refuses, telling you that he wants to keep the land undeveloped so his children and his grandchildren can continue to camp and fish and enjoy the property in its natural state. You increase your offer but your neighbor continues to refuse your entreaties.

What do you do next? You could do nothing and hope that your neighbor doesn't develop the property but then you run the risk that even if he doesn't once he dies his heirs might do so. Most people would impose their Me Perspective, despite what the neighbor was telling them, and continue to raise their offer until they hopefully persuaded him to sell. Even if they could, however, the more he values keeping the land undeveloped the more they would have to pay to get him to sell if they were able to so at all.

Another approach would be to accept his U Perspective and take advantage of the fact that you both share a common interest in keeping the land undeveloped. Once you do that you can use the Collaborate approach to try to come up with a solution that maximizes everyone's interests. You could offer to set up a trust to preserve the land in its natural state perhaps paying your neighbor a reasonable sum of money and granting to him and his heirs the right in perpetuity to camp and fish on the land. That way not only do you both get what you want, but also you are both better off. Your neighbor gets money he would not otherwise have, preserves his land in its natural state, and he and his heirs continue to be able to use the land for camping and fishing. You get to maintain an unobstructed view of the lake and pay much less for that privilege than it would cost to purchase the land if you could actually persuade your neighbor to sell. Without looking at the underlying interests it is difficult to reach any agreement at all. Yet, by using Collaborate techniques to determine each party's interests, a mutually beneficial solution is readily achieved.

Sometimes substantive interests, such as how much money something will cost or how quickly you can get it, are not as important as subjective aspects of someone's U Perspective. People frequently care about the process by which an issue is resolved as much as the substantive interests involved. Unless you satisfy that aspect of their U Perspective you never have the opportunity to address the substantive interests and agreement will elude you. People generally want to feel that the process was fair and that they were allowed to fully participate or that they were treated with sufficient respect.

At times, a party's U Perspective may place more importance on how they are treated, a relationship, or a principle than on the actual substantive outcome. The essence of the U Perspective is that we each have our own unique way of evaluating situations that result from our culture, our upbringing and our past experiences. One person may care deeply about certain specific substantive issues while another may consider the relationship between the parties to be the most important thing.   Moreover, the relative importance of each factor may vary from one situation to another.

People also value things differently based on their circumstances at the moment, both objectively (Collaborate) and subjectively (Convince).   For example, one person might need money today whereas another might be more interested in future income. One party might be willing to take reasonable risks while another might be uncomfortable taking any risk at all. When you Collaborate you are able to find solutions that take advantage of these differences and satisfy each person's most important interests.

When Patricia Hambrecht was President of Harry Winston, she wanted to work out a deal with Carolyn Murphy to be the exclusive spokesperson for their jewelry. Carolyn was then one of the top models in the business and had offers to work for several competing jewelers. However, because of the uniqueness of Harry Winston's merchandise, she wanted to work with them as well. Patricia didn't have the advertising budget to pay Carolyn what she could command elsewhere so she agreed to pay Carolyn partly in cash and partly with jewelry. The cost of the jewelry to Harry Winston is the cost for them to produce it (wholesale) whereas the value of the jewelry to Carolyn Murphy was what she would have to pay to buy it (retail). In addition, Harry Winston receives the publicity benefit of having a top model wearing their jewelry to high profile events. This was a perfect example of the Collaborate technique of taking advantage of value differences, a win/win for both parties.

Even interests that may seem insignificant to you may be very important to the person with whom you are dealing. Carole Cooper described a salary negotiation she was having with the manager of a local television station in the Midwest. Carole was representing a producer from New York. The manager of the station recognized that the producer was talented but was having some problems with her style. He said to Carol, "I know you want more money, but I have some problems with her. She spends a lot of time making personal phone calls." Instead of arguing with him about whether her client did or didn't make too many calls or whether, even if she did, it affected her ability to do her job, Carol replied, "I run an office. I understand. I'll talk to her." And she did. When she and the station manager spoke again a few weeks later he couldn't thank her enough. After that, they were able to agree in short order on a new contract with a significant salary increase for her client. To Carol, it was a little thing but it helped a lot.

To identify whether you should be using Convince or Collaborate try to figure out why someone is taking a particular position. It is often useful to simply ask yourself why and why not. Why is someone asking for something? What interests are being served? Also try to identify obstacles to reaching agreement. Ask yourself why the other person hasn't already agreed to what you are proposing. Keep in mind that someone may have several different interests at any given time. What is frequently forgotten is that people who are purportedly on the same side may also have different interests and different U Perspectives. You may be worried about how much additional work a new project will involve while your boss may be focusing on the increased visibility with top management the project will provide him or her.

Not only do you have to satisfy the people you are dealing with directly, you also have to consider the interests and the U Perspectives of people with whom you may never even speak but who have influence over the process. For instance, the person you are talking with may have a boss currently under consideration for a promotion. Her boss is likely to care more about the immediate impact of what you are discussing than about what may happen five years hence. To get what you want you not only have to consider the interests and U Perspective of the person you are dealing with but those of her boss as well.

Consider the following situation: A husband and wife want to take a vacation together. They have a limited budget and limited amount of time. They can only afford to take one vacation this year and they only have two weeks. She wants to go to Italy because she likes fine dining, sightseeing and shopping.

He wants to go to the Bahamas because he likes to gamble and lie on the beach. The parties could use a Convince approach and decide where to go on vacation based on who cares the most about where they go on vacation, which person has the most power or who can most effectively appeal to emotions such as guilt. There are several Collaborate techniques that can be used to develop a good solution that satisfies both parties' interests. They can trade: this year Italy, next year the Bahamas. Or they can trade one interest off against another. Let's say, in addition, to where they are going to vacation, there is an issue of when they are going to take their vacation. Perhaps she wants to take vacation in the summer and he wants a winter vacation. They could come up with a satisfactory resolution if one of them chose the time and the other chose the place.

Another Collaborate technique is what I refer to as coupling interests. That involves identifying other interests and introducing them into the discussions. For example, the wife might offer to let the husband decide where they go on vacation if he will agree to spend the holidays with her family this year. A third Collaborate technique is expanding your options. The assumption that you only have enough money for one vacation and that you only have two weeks is self-limiting. Those are choices that you make. There are always ways to find more money. There are always ways to get more time off. One possible option for the couple would be to readjust their lifestyle so they could afford to take two vacations. They could work longer hours and earn more money. They could sell items from their attic on eBay. They could give up the lawn service and take care of the gardening themselves. They could offer to work weekends in return for additional time off. It may not be worth it for them to do any of those things but if they don't recognize that they have those choices it limits their options. The most commonly recognized Collaborate technique is to find a different way to satisfy everyone's interests. In this case the couple could look for a vacation spot that offers fine dining, sightseeing, shopping, gambling and nice beaches - Monaco and the French Riviera or Puerto Rico might fill the bill. By focusing on the parties' underlying interests, the couple might be able to find a vacation destination that allows each of them to do all the things they each want to do.

The third step in the Collaborate process is to generate options: an essential element of the problem-solving aspect of this process is to come up with an exhaustive list of possible solutions. From that list you can identify those options which best satisfy all parties' interests and chose from among them. Once you have listed all the available options, everyone still has to agree on one. From the examples we have discussed above, one would think that if we were just creative enough and came up with enough options an obvious best solution would simply emerge. That sometimes occurs. More often than not though, after all the options have been identified, there still needs to be discussion about which one to chose.

There is no single right way to reach a solution from among the multitude of options that satisfy everyone's interests. What works best depends on the type of problem, the relationship of the parties, their respective U Perspectives and the nature of their interests. If you want to Collaborate but the other person doesn't, and his or her interests are diametrically opposed to yours, relying solely on a Collaborate approach is unlikely to work. In that case, you may have to first Convince the person to look at the situation differently by appealing to some aspect of their U Perspectives or Create a totally different approach to dealing with the issue. In fact, in most situations you will want to draw on all three concepts: Convince, Collaborate and Create.

Patricia Hambrecht offered an illustrative example of how the 3 Cs Influencing Method can be used effectively. When she was President of Christie's North America, she needed to use Convince, Collaborate and Create in order to win the right to handle the sale of Van Gogh's painting Portrait of Dr. Gachet. The lawyer for the family that owned the painting made a number of demands but one of the major issues was that he wanted the family to have the absolute right to withdraw the painting from auction if there was a major decline in the stock market. He believed that if the markets declined significantly it would affect the price the painting would bring. Christie's would be spending almost a million dollars to promote the auction so they could not agree to allow the painting to be withdrawn except under the most extreme circumstances.

Patricia first sought to persuade the attorney that even if the markets dropped, it did not necessarily mean that it would hurt the price the painting would command. She pointed to the sale of Van Gogh's Irises for $53.9 million just three weeks after the market crash in 1987. She also explained that withdrawing the painting for any reason would impact the perceived value of the painting. Regardless of what was said, potential buyers would attribute the withdrawal to a problem with the painting, not the state of the financial markets. Nonetheless, Patricia also realized that because of his U Perspective she could not totally persuade him that a major collapse in the stock markets would have no affect on the sale price. Recognizing that, she came up with a solution that satisfied everyone. They agreed that in the event that all three major stock markets - New York, London and Japan - fell by a certain percentage for a certain number of days the owner could withdraw the painting. This satisfied the owner's concern but offered a lot of protection to Christie's. It would have taken a major economic crisis for all three markets to fall at the same time. In fact, the Japanese Exchange did drop by the specified amount shortly before the auction date. If Patricia had agreed to allow the family to withdraw based on a financial setback in any one of those markets the auction would not have proceeded. Yet, because of the way the deal was finally structured, the auction went ahead as scheduled and the painting eventually sold for $82.5 million, the most ever paid for a painting sold at auction at the time.

Understanding someone's U Perspective will help you know not only when the Collaborate approach should be used but also how to most effectively reach an agreement that satisfies everyone's interests as well. Developing, and using, your relationships with others will help facilitate that process.

Chapter 7

Problems that are impossible to solve with one paradigm may be easily solved with a different one.

Joel Barker

Create: Structuring Our Interactions With Others Differently

The Create approach to influencing involves changing the way we structure our interactions with others. Often changing the way we interact with others will change the outcomes we achieve. Many times we are faced with situations where we just don't see a good solution. When that happens, it is usually because we are looking at doing things the way we have done them in the past. If we do things the way we have always done them, we can expect to get the same results that we have always gotten. If we want different results, we need to approach situations differently.

Create works on the theory that how you shape your interactions with others affects the substantive outcome of those exchanges. Bring in different people, create a different type of interaction or perhaps simply deal with someone else in the organization that has a different U Perspective. Sometimes the best solution is to bring your idea to a different organization altogether. Individuals typically have a much greater ability to control how they structure their interactions with others than they realize.

I have long espoused the Create approach in my training classes. When what you are doing isn't taking you where you'd like to go, if you just take a fresh look and approach the situation differently, you will usually be able to come up with a line of attack that will yield better results. After hearing me espouse that philosophy in one of my sessions one of the participants put my belief to the test. She wanted to buy a fuel-efficient hybrid car. Unfortunately for her, at that time so did a lot of others, resulting in hybrids being in short supply. She had placed herself on a waiting list and now, a few months later, her name was about to come up. She asked me how I thought she could negotiate a lower price for the car in light of the fact that they were generally selling at sticker price, with some dealers even asking for a premium above that. I thought and thought but couldn't come up with a way to get the dealer to discount the price as long as he had a waiting list of people willing to purchase the car at full price.

So I went into Create mode. The answer was not to try to get the dealer to offer a lower price, but rather to take advantage of the fact that while this woman wanted a hybrid car she didn't need to have one right away. For her, money was more important than time. The key to garnering a better deal was to find someone who wanted the car immediately and was willing to pay a premium for that privilege. I suggested that she sell her place on the waiting list on eBay and put herself on a new waiting list. She could keep doing that until there was no longer a shortage of hybrid cars. That way she would have the money she earned from selling her place on the waiting list and eventually, once the supply of hybrids caught up to the demand, she would be able to get a better price from the dealer. Instead of trying to negotiate with the dealer at a time when she had very little leverage, the Create approach took advantage of the fact that she had something of value that she could sell - her place on the waiting list.

To obtain the best possible outcomes in your dealings with others make sure that you are dealing with the right people. To determine who to involve, ask yourself these questions: Who are the real decision-makers? Who influences them? How do I get the people who can be the most helpful to want to help me? Donna Lagani, Publishing Director for Cosmopolitan and CosmoGirl magazines understands the importance of working with the right people and offers the following excellent advice, "Never accept a 'no' from someone who could not say yes to what you are asking for!"

Some of the most frustrating interactions you can have are with people that don't have the authority to make a decision and/or who don't care whether or not a satisfactory resolution is reached. When you are faced with that situation you need to harness the U Perspective of the person that you are dealing with in a way that causes him or her to want to help you. Alternatively, you might bypass that individual and go directly to someone who has the authority and who cares. If you seek to do that, though, you need to do so without alienating the person that you are bypassing. Asking that individual for help or advice and gaining their consent to involve someone else is one way to avoid alienating them.

For example, if you are talking with someone who thinks your request is reasonable but says his boss would never agree to it, you could ask him what the two of you could do to convince his boss that what you are suggesting makes sense. By getting him to look at the situation as "we", it changes how he sees it. This is a Create approach that alters the paradigm from one where you are dealing with someone lacking authority and impeding your ability to influence the person who can give you a favorable answer, to one where you and that person are working together to persuade the decision-maker. Every attempt to exert influence is different. No two situations are ever exactly the same. The parties are different. One party may care more or less about what you are doing. Facts have changed. Needs have changed. Times have changed.

When nothing else is different, the simple fact that you have previously dealt with someone before creates a new dynamic. That prior experience, whether positive or negative, now has to be taken into account. Therefore you need to analyze every situation as if it were the first time you had to deal with it. Take a fresh look. Examine your assumptions. Consider whether you are involving all the right people. Determine if other do it differently. Try something else.

Even if you have done your homework, and decided

on an approach that you believe will yield positive results, it may not - because, by definition, someone else with a different U Perspective is involved. So, when something isn't working, try another approach. Maybe you are dealing with the wrong person in the organization or perhaps you are talking with the wrong organization altogether. Maybe you are approaching the people you want to influence in the wrong way or maybe their understanding of the facts is different from yours. When you find yourself in this position, you might consider changing the people on your side of the table. There may be other people in your organization that you could involve. You may want to bring in an expert who supports your position. If there are individuals that you know with a relationship to the people you want to influence, consider getting them involved.

"This is the way we always do it," doesn't have to be the way it is done. Create changes the paradigm to one that gives you an advantage, makes use of the other person's U Perspective, makes it easier to achieve your objectives or, sometimes, just forces everyone to take a fresh look at what is really going on. Create changes the way people look at things. For example, recently I was teaching a class in negotiating for Women Unlimited, an organization that helps corporations develop high potential women executives. During the lunch break one of the students in class asked for my help. One of the assignments for the participants in the program was to interview their company's CEO and report back to the group. This woman, Donna, had been unable to arrange a meeting with her CEO. She had already been rebuffed several times by the CEO's assistant, who said her boss was too busy to meet with her.

The assistant suggested that she interview the Senior Vice President of Human Resources instead. This individual had already tried taking a win/win approach. The assistant told her the CEO didn't have time and, moreover, if he gave an interview to her he would have to do it for others. In an effort to meet those objections she offered to have all the company-sponsored women in the program jointly interview the CEO for no more than twenty minutes. That offer was also rejected.

I suggested she try a different approach altogether, one that took into account the assistant's U Perspective. The assistant viewed her job as protecting the CEO's time, something everyone wanted. As long as the women in the program were viewed as just another group seeking the CEO's time, the assistant would perceive her role as preventing that from happening. So I suggested to Donna that she try to change how the assistant viewed her role in the process. Since people have more than one motivator within the context of their U Perspective, I recommended that Donna explain why it was important for her to speak with the CEO, and ask for the assistant's advice on how best to approach the subject of getting an interview with him. In this way, Donna was able to appeal to the assistant's desire to display her knowledge and be helpful rather than her instinct to protect her boss. By making the assistant an ally in helping her to get the interview, rather than an adversary working against that outcome, Donna was able to change the results. The assistant offered to raise the subject again with the Chairman at an appropriate time, based on her unique understanding of her boss' needs. With the assistant's help, Donna was eventually able to get the desired interview. The real stumbling block here was not the CEO's interests, but the assistant's U Perspective - how she saw her role. The key to overcoming that obstacle was recognizing that there were ways to appeal to the assistant's U Perspective by developing a relationship with her and better understanding her motivations.

While Create requires looking at things differently, it doesn't necessarily require that you come up with a totally new way of dealing with a situation. To Create a new paradigm you have to start by examining the assumptions people bring with them. These assumptions are typically unstated. Often the parties themselves are unaware that they are bringing them to the table. Think about how similar situations have been handled in the past. Look at everyone who is involved and how those individuals interact with each other. Examine the relationships of the people involved. Is there a boss who this person has to answer to? Will their spouse have a say in what is decided? Is this person acting on behalf of someone else? Once you analyze the parties' expectations of how things should proceed, you can consider all the possible ways you might approach a situation differently. Determine each party's interests. Then see if the approach you are taking makes sense in terms of the people and the interests involved or if there might be a better approach.

Within a short time after I first joined Macys as their Vice President of Labor Relations I had the opportunity to use the Create approach. The company had developed a good relationship with its largest union over many years. That union had not had a strike against the company in more than twenty years. In the past, the negotiations had consisted of the union making numerous proposals, often in excess of a hundred, and the company responding one by one to those proposals. Over the course of several months the company would agree to some proposals, tell the union why it couldn't agree to others and compromise on the remaining items. In this game the union was always on the offensive and the company was always on the defensive.

This is not how I had negotiated in the past for other companies nor was it how Macys dealt with its other unions. It seemed obvious to me that this was not the best way to negotiate. But it was the way things had been done for the last twenty years and from the U Perspective of the people running the company it had worked reasonably well in the past. So it took quite a bit of convincing, and the involvement of my new boss who had not been involved in previous labor negotiations, to get everyone to agree that we should try something different this time. In the end we changed the rules and presented the union with a list of proposals of our own – less than a dozen - and modest proposals at that.

Yet this new approach had its intended effect. We spent at least as much time discussing our ten proposals as the union's one hundred plus proposals. Putting forth our own proposals allowed us to go on the offensive at times, which is more fun than always being on the defensive. Most importantly, the union agreed to some of our proposals proving once again that you can't get what you don't ask for. The biggest obstacle to adopting this common sense approach was that it had not ever been done that way before. Once this new strategy was agreed upon it changed how these and future negotiations proceeded.

Changing your approach works particularly well in business because you frequently engage in similar types of transactions. Since each is unique in some way, often the key to getting a better result is to take a new look and not to simply rely on what has been done in the past.

Psychologists say that working at a round or oval table leads to more cooperative discussions, whereas working at a square or rectangular one leads to a more adversarial approach. I doubt that the shape of the table is anywhere near as important as how the parties view their relationship to each other. One of the ways you can Create is to get the other party to change their view of that relationship - figuratively getting the other person to move to your side of the table.

A friend of mine, who is a career counselor, had to Create a different paradigm when she was faced with having to agree on compensation with a friend. She had developed a course on coaching for the continuing education program of a major university. She sought my advice because she felt she was not being fairly paid for her work, which was extremely profitable for the university. The Director of the Continuing Education Program, who was a close friend of hers, had told her that she was already being paid the maximum rate for instructors and that the university couldn't pay her any more. The Director's U Perspective was that if her friend was paid more, to be fair the university would have to raise the other instructors' rates as well.

I initially suggested that my friend see how much

another university would pay her to teach the course and then use that offer to convince the Director that her services were worth more than they were currently paying her. If they refused to match the offer, she could always teach the course elsewhere. She didn't feel comfortable doing that because of her relationship with the Director. We then discussed how to turn that relationship into an advantage, rather than a disadvantage. We decided to explain to the director how much work was involved in preparing and teaching the course. Then, by invoking the U Perspective of a friend, she could seek the Director's help in finding a way for her to be fairly compensated. She did exactly that, changing the paradigm from that of asking her boss for a raise because she could command a higher salary elsewhere, to asking a friend for advice about rectifying an unfair situation.

Because of her U Perspective, the Director couldn't change the hourly rate my friend was being paid. But after hearing about how much preparation was involved and how much material had to be covered, the Director came up with the idea of paying her a fee for her extra preparation time and lengthening the course by two sessions. In this way the Director could pay my friend more without affecting the pay structure of the other instructors. This is an excellent example of how the Create approach can work in conjunction with Convince and Collaborate techniques. First my friend had to Convince the Director that her compensation was not commensurate with the work involved. In addition, she had to Collaborate with the Director in order to find a way to accommodate her interest in being paid more with the Director's interest in not having to pay all the other instructors more money. But had she not first used a Create approach to get the Director to look at the situation through the U Perspective of a friend, rather than that of a boss, she never would have had the opportunity to do so.

Sometimes you won't be able to get what you want by using the Convince or Collaborate approaches. Then your only choices are to Create or to walk away. Bonnie Stone, the Chief Executive Officer of Women In Need, an organization that runs shelters for homeless families, described one such situation. At the time she was Deputy Commissioner for The Human Resources Administration of the City of New York. She had been put in charge of fulfilling the agency's mandate to change the status of home health care workers caring for the disabled and elderly from that of independent contractors to that of employees. This change had to be implemented in order to comply with Federal law.

Bonnie had barely been on the job two days and was attending a meeting to discuss this issue with a coalition of groups representing the disabled and elderly. The leaders of this loose coalition were all severely disabled themselves. They were seated in the audience in their wheelchairs with their respirators and their attendants. The Commissioner logically went through all the reasons why the agency had to make this change and why it would be a good thing for their constituents. The audience refused to go along with what was being proposed. The Commissioner was taken aback by their response and didn't know what to do. So she set up a task force to look at the issue and designated Bonnie to head it.

Bonnie recognized that this group was politically potent and that she needed their cooperation. Fortunately she understood their U Perspective - they viewed this as a control issue, since under the new proposed system their attendants would no longer work directly for them. Most of these individuals were physically powerless. They could not feed or dress themselves. They had little control over their environment. They were not about to give up one of the few things they felt they actually did control.

Bonnie also understood that she would never succeed in reaching an acceptable resolution to this problem in the way she might with other advocacy groups. Anything the government proposed would automatically be deemed unacceptable. Worse yet, even if she could get some of the coalition leaders to agree with her, it wouldn't resolve anything. There was no unified leadership and no agreement among the groups themselves as to how to proceed. The only thing they all agreed on was that they didn't trust the government. Recognizing that underlying each of their U Perspectives was this commonly held belief enabled Bonnie to create a new paradigm. She allowed the coalition itself to come up with the solution. In the end, what they came up with was to have the coalition set up a cooperative in the form of a non-profit corporation that they ran. The cooperative then hired the home care workers as their employees.

Even in the simplest everyday transaction you can use Create if what you are doing is not working. You don't have to be a genius to do so. You just have to be willing to try something different. Claire Irving, a principal in Investigative Consultants LLC, did just that when she couldn't get the customer support that she needed. She had just bought a new PDA. She had been told by the salesperson that the new PDA would work with a particular program she had been using on her old one so that that she would not have to have someone retype all the names and addresses that she had compiled over the years. To do that the salesperson told her she would need to purchase additional software. He suggested that she call customer support to find out what software she needed and where she could buy it.

When Claire got home she called the number the salesperson had given her and inquired about the software needed to run the program on the new PDA. The customer service representative who answered informed her that they did not support that program. She responded that the salesperson had told her when she bought the product that the program would run on the PDA with some additional software. She just wanted to know what she needed to buy. The customer service representative once again unceremoniously informed her that they did not support that program. Back and forth they went like this for several minutes until Claire was ready to blow up. The customer service representative's U Perspective was obviously not about service and was also not about to change. Claire was ready to return the PDA and then she changed the paradigm. Claire asked whether if she hung up and called back she would be reconnected to him. He replied that was unlikely because there were dozens of other customer service representatives working there. Whereupon Claire thanked him, hung up and called back to a different customer service representative.

The person who answered the phone promptly provided her with the information she needed.

Claire wasn't going to get the results she wanted by proceeding the way she had been, so she approached the situation differently. That is essence of what Create is all about. There is almost always another way to go about getting what you want, if you think about things differently. If the traditional way of doing something doesn't work to your best advantage, Create a different approach - one that works better for you.

Part Three:
The U Perspective
At Work

Chapter 8

They may forget what you said, but they will never forget how you made them feel.

Carol Buchner

The Selling Power Of The U Perspective

I have heard that American Express, in order to close a big deal or more likely to ensure that the people working on it feel good about it once it has been completed, sometimes gives a Black Card to the key participants involved in putting the deal together. Ordinarily, in order to qualify for a Black Card, one has to charge $150,000 during the previous year, making it the most prestigious card that American Express offers. Compared to its Platinum cousin, the incremental cost to American Express of offering the Black Card is not significant. The basic costs of most of the services it brings - concierge, airline upgrades etc. - are already in place. The value of the prestige afforded to Black Card holders, though, is considerable.

Whether or not American Express actually offers Black Cards as an inducement to decision-makers of its key customers, doing so would enable American Express to employ the power of the U Perspective to capture key sales. No one needs an American Express Black Card, but taking advantage of how much certain individuals, motivated by status, might want one, would provide an extraordinarily effective sales tool. By the same token, no matter how good your product or service is, failure to take into account your customers' U Perspectives will result in lost sales.

Barbara Jackson once had the enviable task of selecting a resort hotel anywhere in the world as the location for a major corporate event. She was leaning toward the Ritz Carleton on the Hawaiian island of Maui. The purpose of this event was to facilitate a culture shift for her corporate client, which was changing the way it managed its employees from traditional departments to cross-functional teams. Barbara chose Maui because of its unique setting as well as the Hawaiian culture. She had decided to use traditional Hawaiian warrior games to create a sense of teamwork among the members of the new cross functional teams.

Unfortunately, when she arrived on Maui to check out possible locations Barbara was greeted by a monsoon. For the next two days she was stuck inside the hotel with the sales manager who sensed that Hawaii was starting to lose its appeal for her. He assured Barbara that the monsoon season would be long gone by the day of her event and virtually guaranteed her beautiful weather. He used his time with her to describe all the amenities the hotel had to offer: the pool, the restaurants, the spectacular views and the golf courses. He told her that Tiger Woods stays there when he is in Hawaii and mentioned several times that the Cadillac Golf Classic was held there. He even sent her a beautiful pair of Hawaiian pajamas

Despite the monsoon, Barbara kept asking to take a look at the beach. She wanted to make sure it was big enough to hold the games she envisioned. The sales manager eventually confessed that although the hotel had a spectacular ocean view from the twin plateaus it was situated on, it actually only had a twenty by thirty foot beach. Moreover, there was no way he could close it to the other guests so she could hold her games there. He assured her, however, in the inimitable Ritz Carleton style that he would arrange for a suitable beach and for buses to transport her group at no additional charge. The sales manager very nearly lost a million dollar event, all because he didn't bother to determine Barbara's U Perspective. She was determined to hold an authentically Hawaiian event in order to reinforce the cultural theme she was trying to create. Taking buses to the beach to participate in traditional Hawaiian warrior games would hardly have set the right tone. If the Ritz Carleton's beach was not large enough to accommodate the event, she would simply have to hold it elsewhere

What saved the event for the Ritz Carleton was that the sales manager had to leave Barbara to attend to other business. So to entertain this potential million dollar client while she was stuck inside the hotel, he introduced her to the Hawaiian historian that the hotel employed to give talks to guests about local history. In speaking with this historian, Barbara found out that she had been wrong in assuming that traditional Hawaiian warrior games were held on the beach. Tribal warfare did not occur on beaches. Therefore, traditional warrior games were always held "up country." The twin tipped peninsula upon which the hotel was located, above the beach, not only was large enough to accommodate the events she envisioned, but because of its special place in Hawaiian history and breathtaking view, it was the perfect place for what she had in mind.

The sales manager just assumed Barbara's U Perspective was about finding a place in a lovely resort setting, with the fabulous service for which the Ritz Carleton was famous. Because of the way he saw the world, he never even considered the possibility that someone else might have a different U Perspective. Often salespeople approach a customer thinking that they have the answer and that their job is to persuade the customer of the value of their product or service. However, products and services don't have value in the abstract. Their value to the customer is in meeting their specific needs or aspirations at a given moment in time. Once you understand those needs and aspirations you can show how the product or service you are offering is advantageous to this customer in terms of what they care about. In that way you create desire based on a customer's U Perspective.

Too often sales people don't ask or listen. They try to sell what they have, regardless of what the customer wants or needs. Customers like to feel that you have taken the time to listen to them and that you understand their needs. If you allow them to tell you how they see their problems and to share their aspirations, selling becomes a lot easier. Your goal as a salesperson is to discover enough about the customer to be able to match that individual with the right product or service and to show them how what you are offering satisfies their particular needs or aspirations. In other words, before you begin to sell, you need to find out not only what the customer's needs are but what their U Perspective is as well.

Just having the best product is not enough. For certain customers, having a product that is radically better than anything else on the market can even inhibit the sale. Many customers like what they are familiar with and are afraid of change. A radically improved product, even one that objectively better satisfies their needs, may not appeal to them. Why? Because they are comfortable with what they know and fear that they may not be able to master the new technology. They may even worry that the new technology will diminish the value they bring to their organization.

Blackboard Inc., for example, sells software to colleges and universities that allows professors and students to interact online. They can put the course syllabus, reading assignments, homework, lectures, class discussions and tests online. This technology has the potential to dramatically change how universities teach and how students learn. Michael Chasen, Blackboard's CEO, has successfully grown his business to over $170 million dollars in sales, however, by avoiding efforts to sell his software as way to replace the classroom. He was quoted in the New York Times as saying: "How long have people been predicting that higher education was going to experience fundamental change or fall apart? But we are teaching and learning in much the same way we have for centuries. We don't aim to replace the classroom. We're not looking to revolutionize education. We help schools deliver more effectively what they are already good at." Most university faculty believe that what they do, and the way they do it, is uniquely valuable. Any attempt to change the basic way they teach would be greeted with hostility. As a professor, I can tell you unequivocally that Blackboard's success is the result of their keen understanding of academia and the U Perspective of the people who run our colleges and universities.

There are four conditions that a salesperson must satisfy in order to get a customer to buy. I refer to these as **MUST, TRUST, NOW** and **HOW**.

> **MUST** - The customer must want the product or service. They must see a need that would be met or a desire that would be fulfilled by purchasing what you are selling.

> **TRUST** - The customer must trust that you are the right person to buy from.

> **NOW** - The customer must believe that now is the right time to make the purchase.

> **HOW** - The customer must figure out how they can afford what you are selling.

If you meet these four conditions for a customer you can sell them anything. The most important of the four conditions is the first. Must creates the desire for the product or service. That desire is a prerequisite to making the sale. A salesperson can only do that if they understand the customer's U Perspective. That means determining what is important to the customer and what will motivate him or her to buy. Customers often buy based on emotion. When someone wants something, they find reasons to justify buying it. Frequently customers use facts to back up or validate decisions they make for other reasons. Understanding that is essential to being successful as a salesperson.

To persuade a customer that what you are offering is something that they want, you need to discover what motivates them. Different customers are motivated by different things. They may be motivated by a desire to save time or money, make their life easier, improve their health, attract a partner, gain praise, enhance their status, increase their wealth, look and feel better, help their family, be stylish, emulate others, avoid trouble, solve a particular problem, or for a myriad of other reasons. Customers evaluate and react to a salesperson's words by filtering them through their U Perspective. You can enhance your chances of making a sale by drawing on a customer's emotional needs and communicating in terms of those needs. If you know your customers, their needs, their background and their thought processes, selling becomes much easier.

For example, an executive coach I know works with high level executives. She has two different programs that she offers: the CEO program and the Senior Executive program. I am not exactly sure what the difference between the two programs is but it must be significant because the cost of the two programs differs dramatically. Typically companies send executives to meet this coach so they can decide if they want to hire her. The executive also has to decide on the appropriate program. In addition to being an excellent coach, this individual is also an excellent salesperson. She almost always gets her clients to opt for the CEO program. How does she do that? She makes sure that she understands her prospective client's U Perspective.

She described one such individual to me. This prospective client wore an Armani suit and a Rolex watch. He drove a Jaguar and he lived in the "right" neighborhood. He also made sure she knew that. She recognized instantly what his U Perspective was: he was all about status. Did she convince him to choose the CEO program by offering him a discounted rate? No, because that wouldn't have motivated him - lower price equates to lower status. Did she point to all the other famous CEO's who had gone through the program? No, although that would have appealed to his desire for status and probably would have worked as well. What did she do? She told him that he really did not need to spend the extra money for the CEO program because he could probably get everything he needed from the Senior Executive program. After twenty minutes of telling him that he might not really be right for the CEO program, he was begging her to let him participate in that program. Exclusivity appeals to someone with a status based U Perspective. When you understand what motivates someone, you will know how to sell to them.

It is also helpful to find out what is going on in a customer's life. Whatever is most pressing in someone's life at the moment is likely to color their view of the world. Think about someone who is going to a class reunion. If they are bothering to go, they probably want to make just the right impression. If you are a salesperson in a department store you want to know that because it will shape their purchasing behavior. They are going to want to wear something that makes them look great and price is not going to be that important.

Barbara Jackson found herself in just that situation shopping for clothes for her college reunion. She was looking at outfits when a salesperson approached and asked if she was searching for anything in particular. Barbara told her that she needed something for her college reunion that weekend and then described what she had in mind. The salesperson showed her several outfits and they finally found one she loved. She tried it on and it looked really good, but the blouse was a little big. When she couldn't find one in a smaller size, the salesperson told her she would get one from another store and Barbara could pick it up the next day. Unfortunately she had to leave for the reunion the following day, so Barbara told the salesperson she'd just have to make due with the larger size. The salesperson would not hear of it and took the name and address of the hotel where Barbara was going to be staying for the reunion and promised to overnight the blouse so it would be there when she arrived. Barbara was so appreciative that she bought another outfit for the trip. She looked so good at the reunion that she has been a regular customer of this salesperson ever since. That is the selling power that comes with knowing how to use the U Perspective.

Some salespeople make selling look easy. Month after month they outperform their peers even though they are selling the exact same products to the very same customers. How do they do it? They determine what will motivate the customer to buy - not a generic customer but each individual customer. They recognize that every customer is unique. They build a relationship with that customer even if they are only with them for a few minutes. They use whatever time they have with the customer to ask questions and to listen to the response - all for the purpose of determining the customer's U Perspective. Once they understand that, they select products and services that will appeal to that customer and then focus on how those products and services satisfy the customer's U Perspective. Once you do that, not only do your customers buy from you, but they feel good about their decision to buy. They come back again and again and they refer their friends.

Chapter 9

Everything in life is a negotiation of some kind.

Joe Robinson

Negotiating And The U Perspective

How is the 3 Cs Influencing Method, described in Part 2, different when you are negotiating? If you define negotiating broadly, the way I like to define it, as the art of getting what we want from someone else in whatever we do, there is probably little reason to have a separate chapter on negotiating and the U Perspective.

As in other situations, understanding what is important to someone - their U Perspective - enables you to negotiate favorable agreements that maximize what you get at the least cost to you by offering the other person what he or she values most. However, if you view negotiating in the narrower, more traditional sense, as the art of the deal, there is a perceived adversarial aspect to your dealings.

Even if you would like them to be, not all aspects of negotiating can be win/win. Used properly the Collaborate and Create approaches can help you maximize the value of the deal for all of the parties concerned. However, once you do that you still have to allocate that increased value between the parties which normally entails use of the Convince approach. Therefore, most negotiations start off with an adversarial aspect built into each party's U Perspective. That element is heightened where the parties have no prior relationship.

All deals consist of three basic elements - price, timing and specifications. To conclude a deal requires agreement on how much will paid and to whom, who will do what and a timetable for when what has been agreed to will be completed. While there is a tremendous opportunity to make trade-offs and structure a deal in different ways so that each side gets the best possible outcome in terms of what they value most, to the extent that one side gets more money, better quality, or quicker delivery, the burden on the other side is increased. At the same time that you are trying to maximize the benefits of the deal for everyone, you are generally trying to get the most favorable price, timing and specifications that you can.

Sometimes what motivates an individual is trying to get the best possible economic deal - to maximize profits. This is the reasonable person model that traditional economic theory is based upon. Similarly, someone may be motivated to get the best deal in terms of how it will affect them personally - what salespeople refer to as WIIFM (What's In It For Me.) In these types of situations, people's U Perspectives are usually synonymous with what we refer to as their interests. If both parties are motivated by that U Perspective, a Collaborate approach that maximizes everyone's objective interests will usually be the best approach. Many times, though, people are not focused on their objective interests but rather on some emotional need. In those circumstances, before Collaborate can be employed, one must first use the Convince techniques to generate desire by appealing to some other aspect of the person's U Perspective, such as status, fear or greed.

Let's say, for instance, that you are attempting to negotiate a deal with Sally, Director of Production and Distribution, at a company that isn't faring well. An edict has come down from the company's president freezing hiring and salaries - no raises, no promotions, no new hires - No Exceptions! You want to arrange a tie-in deal with this company where you sell their product along with your own. You are willing to pay a premium for their product as long as you can be assured that it will be delivered when and where you need it. You offer Sally a 5% premium if she agrees to provide the product on an as needed basis. This is a good deal for the company because it will allow them to increase their sales as well as their profit margin at a time when they need to do both. Sally initially seems hesitant and asks for additional details about your delivery requirements. You provide the requested information and to move the process along you increase the premium you are offering to 6%. Sally questions whether her company can meet such an aggressive delivery schedule. So you relax your requirements slightly and increase the premium you are willing to pay to 7%, assuming that will enable you to close the deal. Sally asks for more time to study the proposal.

You are at a loss as to what to do. This is an excellent deal for Sally's company and you cannot understand why she is not jumping at this opportunity. Until you understand what is really going on no agreement is going to be reached, or if one is, it will be very expensive. To understand why Sally has not yet agreed to your proposal you need to consider her U Perspective. While this appears to be a very good deal for the company, it is not such a good deal for Sally and her team. They will not only have to work harder to increase production but will have to specially pack and ship products under unusually tight deadlines. In other words, as a result of this deal Sally's life, and the lives of her employees, will become immeasurably more difficult with no prospect of getting more staff or additional financial remuneration. Once you understand her U Perspective, it becomes obvious what needs to be done to gain Sally's agreement. Instead of offering to pay more for the product, you need to offer Sally additional resources to help with fulfillment. For example, you could offer to take responsibility for packing and shipping the product. This would allow Sally to take on this project without drastically increasing her workload and that of her staff.

Adding to the difficulty of negotiating this deal without an accurate understanding of Sally's U Perspective is that she is unlikely to say "no" to the deal because it is good for the company. However, she is also not going to say "yes" to it because it is not good for her. She is simply going to continue to negotiate. Moreover, Sally is unlikely to tell you directly that her primary concern has to do with all the extra work this project will entail. That would sound like she was lazy or wasn't a team player. So, until you figure that out for yourself you'll waste a lot of time and more importantly you may unnecessarily raise your offer because you are assuming that the issue is money. You are focusing on the interests of the company rather than the U Perspectives of the people who are negotiating the deal. In the all too real scenario described above, by the time you determine that the key to reaching an agreement is helping Sally manage her workload, you probably will already have offered to pay more than was necessary. Once you have done that it is unlikely that Sally will subsequently agree to accept less, even though you have resolved her work load concerns.

Often when we negotiate we offer up things that, while costly to us, are not highly valued by the other side. If you don't understand what the other person's U Perspective is, you will typically give away many things that they don't really care about before you actually figure out what is important to them. The problem with that approach is that once you finally determine what is really critical to the other side, and agree to satisfy that interest, you can rarely, if ever, get back what you have already given away.

If you can't understand why an organization is not accepting an offer that would appear to be in their interest, consider the U Perspective of the individuals involved in the deal. Remember, we don't negotiate with organizations, we negotiate with individuals and each individual has his or her own U Perspective. In some instances, what is important to a particular individual may differ substantially from what is in the interest of the organization as a whole. Moreover, there are usually a multitude of different organizational interests involved in most transactions and numerous ways to satisfy them. That needs to be taken into account whenever you negotiate

When you negotiate, always ask yourself why. Why is someone taking a particular position? Why aren't they agreeing to what you have proposed? Why might someone in a position to influence the outcome of the negotiation not want to agree to your proposal? That will help you identify the obstacles to agreement and allow you to make the best use of your available resources to overcome those obstacles.

Bear in mind that not only do you have to satisfy the U Perspective of the people that you are negotiating with directly, but also that of others who can exert influence over the process. Those other individuals may be people with whom you have no direct contact. In fact, you may not even know they are involved. Let's assume that the boss of the person that you are negotiating with expects to be considered for a promotion in the next six months. If you are offering a deal that has significant upfront costs, even though it will result in an excellent return a year or two from now, you are unlikely to reach agreement. In that situation, the person who has to approve the deal, the boss, probably cares more about the immediate impact on his profit and loss statement than about any benefits that might accrue to the company a year or two down the road. Knowing that will inform you as to what you have to do to successfully structure a deal that satisfies the boss' U Perspective. You could, for instance, agree to make an upfront payment to the company in return for a greater percentage of the profits when they are actually earned, thereby making the boss look good now when it is most important to him or her.

Recognizing that people have different U Perspectives allows you to exploit those differences to everyone's benefit.   Let's take the example of two partners seeking to work out an arrangement dividing up the profits from their business. Understanding the differences in their U Perspectives will enable each to maximize what is most important to them. That is the essence of Collaborate and the definition of a true win/win agreement.

In the above example assume that each partner has a different time horizon - one partner needs money now to buy a vacation home while the other is more concerned about saving money for retirement. What would an agreement that takes advantage of the different U Perspectives of those two individuals look like? They might agree to give the partner seeking to buy the vacation home a lump sum payment now in return for the other partner receiving a greater percentage of the profits from the business beginning in ten years when she retires. Alternatively, the partner who wants to buy the vacation home could take a greater percentage of the profits now to cover the mortgage on the vacation home in return for accepting a smaller percentage of the profits in ten years when the other partner intends to retire.

Alternatively, each partner might have a different tolerance for risk. One partner might be open to taking reasonable risks in order to maximize her return while the other partner may not want to take any risk at all. In that case, the partner with the low risk tolerance could be guaranteed a fixed monthly income regardless of the profits actually earned in return for the other partner receiving a greater percentage of the profits in those months when the business makes money.

Another possibility is that each partner may have a different view of the business' future prospects. One partner might believe that earnings have peaked while the other thinks the business will continue to grow more profitable over time. If that were the case, the partner who thinks the business will continue to grow could buy out the other partner based on the current value of the business or she could agree to take a smaller percentage of the profits now in return for a larger percentage of the profits at a specified date in the future.

In each of the above scenarios, by dividing the profits in a way that maximizes what each partner cares most about or in terms of how each views the situation, they are able to reach an agreement that maximizes everyone's interests.

As we demonstrated in Chapter 5, not only do you need to determine someone's U Perspective, you need to bear in mind that once you do, the Convince tools can be used to affect how people perceive the value of what you are offering. How people value what you are offering is shaped by your presentation. Awareness of this psychological phenomenon will not only help you develop your initial proposal using the anchoring concepts we have previously discussed, but will help you develop counter offers and respond to unreasonable positions. This principal will also inform you as to when, and how, to offer concessions.

When you are negotiating anchor high if you are a seller and low if you are a buyer. We refer to this as high/low anchoring. However, anchors have to be reasonable to be accepted. Consider what would happen if you placed your house on the market for $250,000, a price you believe is reasonable, and someone offered you $100,000 to purchase the house. You would dismiss their offer as ridiculous, reject it out of hand and not bother making a counter offer. If, on the other hand, you were offered $240,000, you would likely enter into negotiations with the prospective buyer and would probably end up reaching agreement. Not surprisingly, if the original asking price was $255,000, as long as that was still considered reasonable, you would probably end up selling the house for more. So it is in your interest to anchor your offer or your response at the upper end (seller) or lower end (buyer) of what would be deemed to be reasonable.

How do you determine what is reasonable, normally referred to as the negotiating range? That depends on the nature of the negotiations. In general, you look at what others have agreed to in similar circumstances. What have comparable houses in the area sold for recently?   What have spouses been awarded in alimony in similar situations?   What are workers with equivalent skill and experience paid? What are comparably equipped cars selling for? Getting the answers to those questions will provide you with the negotiating range. There is a wealth of information available on the internet to help you determine the negotiating ranges for salaries, homes and cars. You can also get data from knowledgeable people in the field such as real estate brokers, divorce lawyers and corporate recruiters. When you are doing a business deal you can look to various methods of valuation as well as what people who have recently engaged in similar transactions have agreed to.

Who makes the first proposal can also play a critical role in determining what anchor the parties will eventually decide to use. So who should go first? If you are able to determine with a fair degree of certainty what the reasonable range of possible outcomes is, then you should make the initial proposal. That way you set the anchor. This is normally the situation when you are buying a car. If you have done your homework, you know what the dealer paid for the car. While the dealer will seek to use the sticker price as the anchor, if you start with the dealers cost and negotiate up from that you are almost certain to get a better price than if you allow the car dealer to start from the sticker price and negotiate down

In a situation where the range of possible outcomes is less clear, such as in employment situations, it is better to let the other side make the initial offer. Otherwise what you propose may be less than the other side might have offered had you allowed them to go first. Moreover, if you initially ask for too much it may result in a premature termination of the discussion. This creates a no win situation. If you make the first offer, you will either end up asking for too little or too much. The exception to this rule is when the person you are negotiating with is already looking at a low anchor. In that case you have to affirmatively take action to change their point of reference.

For example, if your current salary is significantly

below market and your prospective employer knows what you are earning, you do not want the employer to make the first offer. If they do, they will use your below market salary as their anchor. You need to change how they view the situation.   One way to do that is to provide them with information as to the market rate for the position and let them know that you expect to receive a competitive salary. That way the market rate becomes the anchor. As discussed previously, another way to change their anchor is to obtain another offer. The other offer then automatically becomes the new anchor.

When you negotiate you are sometimes faced with someone who anchors an offer too high or too low. If that occurs, the best response is to refuse to accept their anchor. If you respond to an unreasonable anchor with a reasonable counter-offer you will eventually find that you are either paying too much or that you can not reach a fair agreement. This results from how we normally negotiate and general concepts of fairness that pervade our U Perspectives. There is a tendency when we negotiate to resolve differences in the end by splitting the difference. Therefore if someone anchors too high and you accept that as a legitimate starting point, even though you recognize that it is unreasonable, you will still end up offering at some point to split the difference, resulting in a bad deal for you. In other words, if you begin negotiating from an unreasonable anchor the other side has more room to make concessions and will typically end up better off than if you insist on a reasonable offer to begin with.

Let's look at what might happen if you responded to the offer of $100,000 to buy your house by countering with a reasonable offer of $240,000, the very bottom of the negotiating range. If the other party now comes back with an offer of $225,000, the conversation might proceed as follows:

You:	I won't go below $240,000
Buyer:	Tell you what I am going to do, I'll offer you $230,000 but that is it.
You:	The house is worth $240,000
Buyer:	Look I've made a big concession to you. We are not that far apart. Why don't we just split the difference?
You:	$240,000 is a fair price.
Buyer:	You're being unreasonable. I am willing to move. Meet me halfway.

Eventually either you give in, and sell the house for less than $240,000, rationalizing that it is not that much of a difference or you don't make the sale. The best response to an offer that is not reasonable is to simply reject it. Insist that you get a fair offer to begin with or refuse to consider it. There are many ways you can do this and still keep the door open for the other person to come back with a reasonable offer. You can ask them to justify how they came up with the offer and when they can't provide you with a good rationale, ask them to go back and rethink their offer. You can simply tell them you would "be happy to consider a reasonable offer if they come back to you with one, but you can't even consider what they are offering." If you are asked what you are looking for, you can respond that the asking price was fair and that is what you are looking for. Whatever you do, you can not allow someone to get away with setting an unreasonable anchor as the starting point for the negotiations. You will end up paying too much, getting too little or giving up too much just to get an agreement. As you can see, value is often as much psychological as it is real.

High/low anchoring, of the type described above, is only one form of anchoring. There is also what I refer to as "concept anchoring." This can best be illustrated by the following example: say you are seeking money for a new project at work. You go to the person who is in charge of funding these types of projects and ask for $100,000 to get the project up and running. She is convinced that the project is worthwhile but she tells you that she can only free up $60,000 from the budget to fund it. This is a typical high/low anchoring and at best you are likely to get the project funded for less than the full amount you are seeking. By using concept anchoring there is the possibility of getting the full funding you have requested. Concept anchoring requires changing the focus of the discussions by anchoring in a totally different way. In this instance, instead of discussing available budget you want to refocus the discussion on the revenue the project will generate. You might do that by saying something like, "I really appreciate your support. Sixty thousand dollars would allow me to get the project up and running in a year. Thereafter we would be able to generate approximately $20,000 a month in additional revenue. However, if you can give me $100,000 we will be able to get the project going in six months and by the end of the year one it will already have paid for itself." By changing the focus of the discussions from available budget to potential revenue, you change the way the other person views the situation and are more likely to achieve the outcome you are seeking.

Another form of anchoring is what I call "options anchoring." When you use options anchoring you give the other person a choice. For example, I can sell you top of the line goods at a premium price with quick delivery, medium quality goods at a reasonable price with an average delivery time or fair quality goods at discounted price with delivery when I can. If you have set the specific terms of each offer in a way that yields you the same profit you do not care which offer the other person's prefers. Even though they may seek to negotiate better terms for whichever offer they chose the starting point will be your anchor. The beauty of this form of anchoring is that while you have set the anchor, because you have given the other party a choice they feel that they are in control of process.

In the same way, how you make concessions affects how someone values those concessions. Timing your concessions properly is important. Making concessions before the other side is ready to respond in kind will only result in raising their expectations. How much time is necessary before you give ground on a particular issue? That depends on the relationship between the parties and what is at stake. A good rule of thumb, however, is the more important the issue is to the other person, the more time you should spend just talking about it before making any concessions. It is usually best to discuss all the issues and to listen carefully to what the other side says before you offer any concessions. That way you will have a better understanding of what is important to them. It is also generally a good idea when you make a significant concession to ask for something in return. Even if you don't get what you are asking for the other party will value the concession more because you sought something in return.

Thus, how you negotiate and how you grant concessions affects how the other side perceives the value of that concession. That is what Convince is about - enhancing the perceived value of what you are offering. For example, if you advertise an antique desk in the newspaper for one thousand dollars and first thing the next morning someone comes by and offers to pay you one thousand dollars for the desk, your immediate reaction will be that you priced it too low. But if the buyer tries to get you to sell the desk for nine hundred dollars, even if you remain firm and she eventually agrees to pay you nine hundred and fifty dollars, you will feel like you negotiated a good price.

Negotiating is a process and you generally can not short-circuit that process. Cultural norms impact our U Perspective in terms of what we expect when we negotiate. In most countries that means when we negotiate there is expected to be a give and take. Whomever you are negotiating with expects you to be willing to improve your initial offer at least a little. Failure to do that typically results in the other party feeling that you are not negotiating in good faith. Similarly, if one party makes a concession, the other is usually expected to respond in kind. Each time one of the parties makes a concession, you get closer to an agreement. Concessions can also be used when the negotiations begin to bog down or when you cannot agree on a particular issue. To maximize value to each side use the Collaborate technique as discussed above to identify difference in how the parties value the items being discussed. Then, based on each party's U Perspective, find ways to give each side what they value most.

Be careful not to make concessions too easily even on matters that are not really important to you. Most people do not sufficiently value what they get with little effort. Granting concessions too quickly makes them seem insignificant, and people have short memories. Just because you agree to something early on doesn't mean that the other side will remember this later when the negotiations hit a rough spot. Therefore, it is usually best not to make concessions too early or too readily. Always treat what you are giving as something that is important to you. Otherwise your gesture will not have its desired effect. If what you are offering is important to the other side it ought to be important to you. Treat it that way.

In addition, concessions should never be used in a way that undermines your negotiating theme. Changes in your position need to have a reasonable justification or the other side will believe your initial position was not genuine and your credibility will be damaged. You can use concessions to demonstrate that you have heard what the other side has said. You can justify a change in your position as an attempt to accommodate the other party's interests or based on new information that the other side has provided to you. Alternatively, changes in your position can be justified by introducing a new party into the negotiations such as a mediator or someone who has a particular expertise.

It is also generally a good idea to vary your use of concessions. Sometimes you can simply concede on a given point and follow up with a request for something else. Other times you might offer to trade one thing directly for another. Occasionally you may concede something simply to gain some goodwill.

Finally, always ask for more than you expect to get and keep something in reserve to Convince the other person to close the deal. As the process moves toward its conclusion concessions can be used to maximum effect. At the conclusion of a deal, you may be able to gain something that would have been impossible to obtain earlier in the process. Over time the U Perspective of the parties will change. The longer the negotiations go on, up to a point, the greater everyone's stake in reaching an agreement becomes. Moreover, granting concessions toward the end of the negotiations effectively allows the other side to go away feeling like they "won." The optimal outcome in any negotiations is being able to Convince people to do what you want, yet allow them to walk away feeling good about the resulting agreement.

Failure to find out what someone's U Perspective is can result in misunderstandings and missed opportunities. In the training business, speakers frequently hire others to prepare their slides and write their workbooks. There are a number of writers who specialize in providing such services. One such writer described a situation where the failure to listen, and understand her U Perspective, not only cost the speaker who hired her money but soured their relation to such an extent that she will no longer work for him.

At his request, she had agreed to rework his presentation for an upcoming event and to write an accompanying workbook. When they discussed her fee for the project she clearly indicated that it would depend on how much work was involved but that she thought it would be somewhere between $2,500 and $3,000. As it turned out the project entailed a lot more work than she had anticipated. When it was completed, the writer informed the speaker that she was going to charge him $3,000 for her work. His recollection of their initial conversation was that the price was to be $2,500 and, in fact, he told her he had already asked his bookkeeper draw up the check. An argument ensued.

The writer had been counting on that payment. Because she desperately needed the money to pay some bills, the writer finally agreed to accept $2,500 but only if the check was sent out right away. Apparently, not only did the speaker not hear that, but he was completely oblivious to her U Perspective - getting the money immediately was more important to her than getting the full amount she believed was due her. About a month and many unreturned phone calls later, the writer finally got a check for $3,000. Even though she ultimately was paid the full amount she sought, because the speaker failed to take her U Perspective into account, despite being explicitly told what was important to her, he not only ended up paying more money but he irreparably damaged his relationship with the writer.

If you can figure out someone's U Perspective, you can determine what it is that will most effectively motivate them to want to reach an agreement with you. You will be able to focus your offer on those things that the other side truly values, enhance the perceived value of what you are offering using the Convince tools, and use differences in how the parties' value things to Collaborate effectively and arrive at win/win agreements. You will be able to use Create to determine who to involve and select the best party to do the deal with. When you reach an impasse you will be able to appeal to the other person's U Perspective to break the logjam. In short, you will be able to effectively negotiate to get what you want, at the least cost to you.

Chapter 10

Businesses planned for service are apt to succeed; businesses planned for profit are apt to fail.

Nicholas Murray Butler

High Performance Customer Service

Not too long ago, I found myself standing at an airline counter waiting while the customer ahead of me was checking his bags and I overheard him say to the ticket agent, "I'd like that bag to go to New York, that one to Chicago and the third to Miami." The agent looked at him in disbelief and said, "That's ridiculous. I can't do that." The customer, with just a touch of sarcasm, replied, "Why not?" You did it last week."

Most customers share certain expectations about the products and services that they purchase. They expect the product or service to satisfy a perceived need or desire, to be priced fairly, to reliably deliver the promised benefits, and to do so on a timely basis. How important each of those expectations is to them will vary from customer to customer. Those who care most about price may not expect a high level of service. Others care most about time or ease of use; they want things to be simple to use and to work well the first time and every time thereafter. What a particular customer cares about may differ depending on the product or service involved.

Good customer service requires systems that are customer focused and employees that are trained to put the customers' needs as their top priority. The surest way to lose customers is to focus on your needs rather than those of the customer. Customer-focused organizations create systems designed to make the customer's life easier and their interactions with the organization more enjoyable. They know that customers hate it when you make them wait, seem not to care, make them repeat information they have previously provided, don't focus immediately on their problem, are unable to help them or simply pass them off to someone else. In customer-focused organizations, employees are trained to avoid doing things that irritate customers. They are trained to treat customers the way the customer wants to be treated.

Most organizations, on the other hand, develop their procedures focusing on interests, such as facilitating financial reporting or managing inventory, that have nothing at all to do with improving the customer's experience. Ultimately, it is not the systems but rather the people who operate those systems, and their understanding of the customers' U Perspectives, that ensure a high level of customer service.

Barbara described an all too common instance where a manager allowed the company's IT systems to prevent her needs as a customer from being satisfied. Barbara had purchased two oversized umbrellas, but as it turned out she didn't need them and wanted to return them. She had her receipt and assumed that returning the items would not be a problem. When she got to the store however, for some reason the computer wouldn't accept the return. The salesperson didn't know what to do so he called his manager over. She couldn't figure out what to do either. Instead of focusing on the customer's needs, the manager told Barbara that there was nothing she could do. Barbara insisted that they take back the unopened goods. She had her receipt and the store's policy allowed returns within 30 days. The manager said the best she could do was to give her a store credit which Barbara was willing to accept. However, because the register would not accept the return, the manager insisted that Barbara use the credit that day and use it in the same department because otherwise the transaction would not register properly in their system. Needless to say, Barbara had no need for more umbrellas and left the store unhappy with the two umbrellas in tow. Even though she ultimately was able to return the umbrellas at a different store location, she no longer shops at that department store.

Customers don't care about company systems. They don't care about company rules. What they care about is having their problems solved and being treated well in the process. That is their U Perspective. Good customer service means finding ways to overcome the obstacles created by a company's systems if they prevent you from satisfying the customer.

Customer service oriented employees understand

that "We can't do it that way" is never something a customer wants to hear, unless it is followed by "but we can accomplish what you want if we do it this way." A colleague of mine who works from home was seeking to find ways to reduce his phone bill. He had six different lines and several services which he used for a variety of different business purposes. A telecom representative with whom he spoke assured him that he would be able to save money by consolidating all his services with their company. The price he was quoted for a package combining all his current services with them was extremely favorable. For most of the services it provided a substantial savings. He, however, had an extremely inexpensive international long distance rate package that he had signed up for years earlier, one that this company could not come close to matching. The telecom representative informed him that to get the favorable package that the company was offering international long distance had to be included. That almost ended the conversation because this individual made a lot of overseas calls and was not about to give up the exceedingly good deal he currently had for international long distance.

The telecom representative listened and understood this customer's U Perspective. He found a way of including as part of the package an international long distance service. The international long distance feature he suggested only charged the customer when the services were actually used and then only on the line designated, which the representative suggested be the line this person used for his fax. That satisfied the company's requirements for eligibility for this particular package but allowed the customer to keep his preferred international long distance service. That is good customer service. If the rules don't readily allow you to meet reasonable customer expectations use the Create techniques to find a different way to satisfy the customer's U Perspective.

Good customer service is not only about providing the customer with the products and the services they want in the way that they want them but also in dealing with customer problems when things don't go as expected. No matter how hard you try, from time to time things go wrong in every business. What brings the customers back is how you treat them when they do.

More than anything else, good customer service is about perception. How customers perceive their treatment depends on their U Perspective. When you don't satisfy a customer's U Perspective they don't return. It doesn't matter that you fixed the problem. All that matters is how the customers feel when they leave. If they don't feel that they were treated well, they will not come back. Customers may not always be right but they can always take their business elsewhere.

Even the best products and services will not meet customer expectations one hundred percent of the time. Sometimes things happen that are beyond your control. Sometimes the customer does not follow instructions. Sometimes the customer's expectations are not realistic. Sometimes people make mistakes. And sometimes things just don't work the way they are supposed to. No matter what has occurred, good customer service means making it right for the customer. To make a customer happy, particularly when something goes wrong, you have to understand what that person cares about.

When things go wrong you often find yourself dealing with an angry customer. At the very least the customer is probably upset and for good reason. Regardless of who is at fault, the customer's expectations have not been met. This is not what the customer wanted when he or she chose your organization to do business with. Whether you agree with it or not, that is the customer's U Perspective. You ignore it at your peril.

When someone is upset they want to know that you care. Acknowledge those feelings immediately. The U Perspective of many customers requires that someone accept responsibility for the fact that what they purchased has not performed the way they expected it to. Don't be afraid to say "I'm sorry." Saying "I'm sorry" does not have to mean that your organization did something wrong. You can say you are sorry that the customer has been inconvenienced or that the product/service did not meet the customer's expectations. You also show customers that you care by listening to them and agreeing with them.

You can never win by arguing with a customer. Even if you win the argument you will lose the customer. If the organization did not do anything wrong, you can still agree that the customer is upset or has been inconvenienced. Customers want to feel that they are being heard. Sometimes they just need to vent. Visibly demonstrating that you are listening to the customer serves an important function. It shows that you care.

The power of the U Perspective to create customer

loyalty comes from understanding how customers perceive a situation and how they will react to what you say and do, considering how they see things. Therefore, whenever a customer's expectations are not met a problem exists that needs to be addressed. It doesn't matter if you are not at fault or even if the customer's expectations are not reasonable. Because the customer perceives that a problem exists, you have to either fix the problem or change the perception.

Moreover, since customer service is about the customer's perceptions, just fixing the perceived problem is not enough. You also have to fix the relationship. Our U Perspective is different when we are dealing with people that we know and like than when we are dealing with strangers. That is why it is so important to create a relationship with your customers. A customer is much less likely to take his or her business to a competitor if the customer has a personal relationship with someone in the organization. They need to change their interaction with the customer from an impersonal transaction with a stranger into a personal one with someone the customer knows and likes.

In addition to creating a relationship with your customers, good customer service requires showing your customer's that you appreciate them. Part of every customers U Perspective is not wanting to feel that they are being taken for granted. Employees should thank their customers often, verbally, in writing, by e-mail and sometimes with a gift.

Customers want to feel that they come first. The following tips are helpful for providing good customer service. If you are working on something else when you are contacted by a customer, put it away. Give the customer your complete attention. If you are dealing with a customer on the phone, avoid placing the customer on hold unless absolutely necessary and for as brief a time as possible. If you have to consult with someone else or have to place a customer on hold while you try to resolve their problem, ask their permission first, check back with them frequently and tell the customer what you are doing for them while they are on hold. If you can't solve the problem immediately, tell the customer what you are going to do for them, do it, and then report back to the customer when it's done. And never simply pass the customer on to someone else without staying involved and retaining ownership of the transaction.

The difference between success and failure in today's business environment is customer service. It is the only advantage that lasts. If you have the best product or service, someone inevitably will come up with one that is a little better or simply improves on yours. If you provide the lowest priced product or service sooner or later someone will find a way to sell something similar for slightly less. However, if you provide high performance customer service, your customers will not leave you just because there is a similar product or service that may be just a little bit cheaper or a little bit better. Moreover, if you consistently provide high performance customer service, customers will buy additional products and services and refer other customers to you.

Good customer service is not slogans. It is not simply always giving the customer everything they ask for. It is not "The customer is always right."

High performance customer service is ensuring that customers feel good about being your customer. It requires not just solving the customer's immediate problem but also setting up the conditions for that customer to continue doing business with you, purchasing additional products and services. By paying close attention to each customer's U Perspective and satisfying it you can provide customer service that creates loyal customers who keep coming back.

Chapter 11

Nothing succeeds like the appearance of success.

Christopher Lasch

Careers: Landing The Job, Getting The Promotion, And Managing Up

---

Jane was interviewing for a job as the Senior Vice President of Human Resources for a major manufacturing organization. She had done her homework. The company was facing a number of organizational challenges which she was well qualified to address. Technology changes and an extremely competitive business environment required the company to transform the way it did business. Jane had spent the last several years managing similar organizational changes. She was fully prepared to show her prospective boss how valuable that experience would be to his organization as it sought to address those challenges. Yet, when she was interviewed by her prospective boss, he spent most of the time asking about her experience with compliance issues, due to a pending lawsuit that the company was embroiled in. Jane answered his questions and demonstrated that she was fully capable of resolving those issues which, in fact, were fairly straight forward. However, she kept trying to return the focus of the interview to her qualifications to handle the more important organizational change issues that the company needed to address. Despite the fact that Jane was objectively probably the best qualified candidate for the position she didn't get the job.

Some people seem to be able to continuously move forward in their careers, gaining promotions and getting whatever jobs they seek. Other people never seem to be able to gain any career traction. The difference lies in knowing how to address the U Perspectives of the people in positions to hire and promote them.

What determines why one person is selected for a job and another is not? Most people answer that question by citing qualifications. The person with the most relevant skills and experience gets the job, right? Like most people, if that is how you answered that question, you would be wrong. If someone is able to obtain a job interview, they are probably qualified to do the job. However so is everyone else that gets called in to be interviewed. In fact, unless it is a preliminary interview, recruiters don't waste their time unless they are fairly certain, based on the information they have, that the applicant can do the job. The key to being selected for a job is distinguishing yourself from all of the other qualified candidates.

Standing out from the crowd has more to do with your understanding of the employer's U Perspective than it does with your qualifications. Employers are not looking for the candidate with the best qualifications. There is no such thing as the best qualified candidate in the abstract. There is only the best candidate for a particular job. To show that you are the right person for the job that you are seeking requires an understanding of the U Perspective of the people involved in making the decision to hire or promote you.

While in most organizations there is a common set of shared values referred to as the organization's culture, you don't interview with an organization. You interview with individuals. For most jobs, you will have to interview with more than one person. Each person who interviews you sees the job somewhat differently. They define the perfect candidate as the perfect candidate for them. To Convince an interviewer that you are the right person for the job, you need to figure out what the interviewer cares about.

How each person defines the perfect candidate usually can be found in the answer to the question "What can this candidate do for me?" Individuals tend to see the answer to that question differently depending on their role in the organization. Someone from Human Resources will have a different U Perspective than someone in Finance and both will differ from that of your future boss as to what they are looking for in a job candidate.

The Human Resources executive is usually looking for the easy, obvious choice - someone who will be readily accepted by everyone involved. That way the Human Resources executive can fill the position quickly and move on to other work. He or she also usually doesn't want to take risks. The Human Resources executive needs to be able to the articulate reasons why you are the best candidate for the job. If a candidate has all the right skills and experience, and fails, no one will blame him or her for recruiting someone who was clearly wrong for the job. On the other hand, if that Human Resources executive favors someone who doesn't fit the job specifications exactly, even if the candidate is otherwise outstanding, and it doesn't work out, the Human Resources executive is likely to face criticism. So, typically, Human Resources executives opt for the safe choice. When you interview with a Human Resources executive demonstrate how you meet all the important qualifications for the job. Be prepared with specific examples of things that you have done in the past that relate to the types of problems the company is currently facing.

Sometimes a Finance executive will be involved in the hiring process. What is their U Perspective? The Finance executive wants someone who they will be able to work with - someone who knows how to stay on budget and help reduce expenses or generate revenues. Those are the skills you want to emphasize if you happen to be interviewing with a Finance executive.

The hiring manager, your future boss, is looking for someone who can help solve his or her most pressing problems, whatever they are. The hiring manager has immediate needs and wants someone to help take care of those needs. Hiring managers are most likely to be focused on whatever they deem to be the most significant problem they face at that moment. They want someone that can have an immediate impact.

Therefore, the most important question you can ask your prospective boss is, "What is it at work that keeps you up at night?" The answer to that question will help you determine the hiring manager's U Perspective. That is what you should focus on. If you can help the interviewer deal with those issues, you have gone a long way toward getting the job.

While you are the same person, with the same skills, experience and personal qualities no matter who is interviewing you, what you chose to emphasize makes all the difference in the world. Remember each person you interview with views the job being filled slightly differently, based on how they interact with that position. That is why it is their U Perspective. When you are talking about your ability to do the job, how you are seen by the interviewer depends on what you choose to emphasize. Focus on what is important to the person interviewing you.

Always exhibit a positive attitude. Interviewers, almost without exception, are looking to hire individuals who are enthusiastic and who really want the job. That is a nearly universal aspect of their U Perspective. So, in addition to focusing on the skills each interviewer cares about most, show that you really want the job. Ask for it. The same is true about promotions. Between candidates under consideration for a promotion, and there is usually more than one, the candidate who gets the promotion more often than not is the one that wants it the most and demonstrates that to those making the decision.

Another critical aspect of moving forward in your career is the ability to gain the support of your boss and other superiors. You need that support to get the resources necessary to be successful as well as assignments that will move your career forward. The process of gaining that support is sometimes referred to as managing up. I prefer to call it managing their U Perspectives.

A particularly effective way to manage up is to allow your boss to believe that what you want to do is really his or her idea. One way to do that is to use something your boss has said and remind him or her that what you are suggesting is a result of that idea. If a boss thinks something is their idea, they will no doubt think it is a good one and support it. While that may sound manipulative, the U Perspective of many bosses includes some variant of "I know best, which is why I'm the boss." If that accurately describes your boss' U Perspective, you can't change it, so your success depends on harnessing it to your advantage. Managing up is getting to know your boss' U Perspective and aligning what you want with what your boss wants. Make his or her priorities your priorities. You won't be able to accomplish what you want unless your boss sees it as in some way furthering something he or she wants.

It is also important to understand how your boss views your success. Some bosses consider the number of their subordinates that have gone on to be successful elsewhere as positive reflection on their abilities. Others, however, jealously guard their status and react negatively whenever they perceive a subordinate as threatening to outshine them in any way. It is not uncommon for the latter type of boss to have a falling out with any subordinate who show signs of independent success. Donald Trump's recent firing of his Apprentice co-star would seem to fall into this category as does Michael Eisner's falling out with his heir apparent Jeffrey Katzenberg at Disney. Even Tiger Woods seems to have resented the independent celebrity status his long time caddy, Mike Cowan, was achieving and fired him in 1999. If you want to move your career forward, seek to determine the U Perspective of a prospective boss before you accept a position and look for one that falls into the former category. If your boss is likely to be threatened by your success avoid the spotlight and be careful to publicly give your boss credit for helping achieve those successes. Do not linger too long under that type of boss' tutelage.

Part of a person's U Perspective is how they like things to be presented to them. Understanding how to best present information to your superiors is another key to career success. Your superiors are more likely to be receptive to what you are saying and to give you what you want if you communicate with them in a way that they are comfortable with. Some executives want a detailed analysis while others prefer just the executive summary. Some focus on their budget while others focus on revenue opportunities. Show how what you want is consistent with what your superiors care about and you are on your way to gaining their support. As we discussed in Chapter 5, use the language that your superiors use and present information in the ways that they are used to seeing it, for example PowerPoint presentations, using consultant recommendations, or confidential memorandums.

Getting the job, being promoted and managing up to get the resources and assignments that you seek are what will propel your career forward. Understanding the U Perspectives of your superiors and harnessing their interest and values to gain their support will help you do just that.

Chapter 12

Good management is the art of making problems so interesting and their solutions so constructive that everyone wants to get to work and deal with them.

Paul Hawken

The U Perspective As A Management Tool

Good managers recognize that each employee is motivated by different things and that even the same person will need to be motivated differently at different times. The importance of distinctions in what motivates different individuals comes into play in every aspect of an employee's career, beginning with the hiring process. Organizations want to hire research chemists who are motivated by intellectual challenge while salespeople are selected who are primarily motivated by money and success. If we want to build a team environment we look for people motivated by social acceptance and the desire to be part of a team. Law firms and investment banks, on the other hand, seek to foster an environment that rewards star performers. Because only a handful of those hired are eventually promoted to be partners in those firms, competitiveness is a quality prized in new hires.

The need to understand what motivates an employee does not end once an individual is hired. Recognizing what motivates employees enables managers to push them to provide peak performance and helps them prevent conflicts between employees. Many executive coaches will tell you that the primary reason for conflict in the workplace is a lack of communication. While good communication is important, it is not enough to maintain an efficient workplace. You need to understand each employee's U Perspective as well. Workplace conflict often results from the fact that different departments have different goals. The Finance Department may be judged based on their ability to reduce costs while the Marketing Department may have their bonuses determined by how successful the company has been at increasing market share. Moreover, individuals see the world differently, based on their personalities and past experiences. To be able to successfully manage employees who have different goals and/or who see the world differently requires more than just better communications.

Managers can satisfy an employee's U Perspective through a variety of means - monetary rewards, promotions, recognition, fear, creating a challenging work environment or encouraging positive social interactions with their peers, to name just a few. Individuals will respond differently to each of those motivational tools based on their own personal values and life experiences. Similarly, different departments may need to use distinct motivational tools because salespeople, for example, typically are motivated differently than are accountants. Moreover, at any given time, some of these motivational tools may be better suited to an organization's particular needs than others.

Successful organizations both hire and motivate employees in ways that are consistent with the type of corporate culture they wish to create. They use the interviewing process to identify employees whose U Perspectives they believe will allow them to fit into that culture. Their motivational tools encourage the types of behavior they seek to cultivate. Providing recognition for good work will only go so far, if monetary rewards and promotions do not follow. Similarly, simply paying everyone more money may not produce the results you seek. If rewards are not based on differences in performance, it may result in negative feelings among the better producers and actually de-motivate them.

When compensation systems and recognition do not support each other employees become confused about what is expected from them. That is why, for example, when call centers exhort employees to provide good customer service and recognize employees who receive customer compliments, but pay and/or discipline employees based on the number of calls they handle, the company ends up with both unhappy customers and unhappy employees. An employee who spends the time necessary to satisfy a customer's needs will be penalized because the pay system values productivity more than customer satisfaction. This leaves employees with the choice of either satisfying customers or being considered productive, a lose/lose situation for the employee and the company. Yet many organizations do just that because they fail to take into account the U Perspectives of their employees and that of their customers when they design their policies and procedures.

Good managers spend most of their time helping their good employees become better. These are the employees who will make you successful. Most managers, however, spend much of their time dealing with those employees that are causing problems. The best way to deal with problem employees is not to hire them in the first place. If you use the proper screening tools, particularly using the interview process to determine an employee's U Perspective, it is not difficult to spot those that are likely to become problems. Failing that, you need to motivate those employees to get them working productively or else fire them so that you can spend your time focusing on building your business.

Difficult or problem employees can be understood and dealt with in terms of their U Perspectives. Often problem employees are considered problems because they try to satisfy their U Perspectives in ways that other people find unacceptable. A natural response is to assume that these employees don't understand that their behavior is dysfunctional. Managers think that if only they take the time and communicate their needs better the problem will be resolved. Unfortunately, this fails to take into account that for many difficult employees the problem behavior is not a problem for them – only those with whom they work.

In terms of the problem employee's U Perspective, there is no incentive for them to change their behavior just because the manager communicates his or her needs more clearly. Since most of us do not like working with or being around difficult people, we often allow these individuals to get their way on issues rather than having to deal with them. Acceding to bad behavior does not, however, resolve the problem. In fact, it encourages more of the same behavior. Neither is the answer to confront these individuals whenever they behave in ways that you don't like. Even if you wanted to do that it would become a full time job. Moreover, it would probably not substantially change their behavior. The key to changing their behavior lies in understanding their U Perspective. Once you comprehend how these individuals see a situation you can find ways to motivate them to do what you want, by appealing to what motivates them rather than erroneously assuming that they are motivated by the same things that motivate most of the rest of the organization.

The behavior of several common types of difficult employees that you encounter in the workplace can be explained by examining their U Perspective. Since every person's U Perspective is individual to them, even if someone's behavior seems to fit within one of these categories of difficult employees, the suggested approaches for dealing with them cannot simply be mechanically applied. Understanding someone's U Perspective requires understanding them. That entails observing them, listening to them and tailoring your response specifically to what you see and hear. How you deal with difficult employees, to some extent, will depend on whether they are your subordinates, your peers or employees who report to someone else. However, understanding their U Perspective will enable you to determine the appropriate approach, regardless of whether you are in a position to formally evaluate their performance and deal with it directly.

The same basic guidelines apply to handling difficult employees even when they don't report to you. Use both positive and negative reinforcement. Seek feedback. Listen. Try to understand their U Perspective and don't expect them to see things the same way you do. Channel their U Perspective in productive ways. Recognize that you can't change people; you can only change their behavior. Take timely action. Set expectations. Spell out consequences for failing to change their behavior. Remain unemotional. Document what they do and what they say. Allow people to save face. Finally, do not spend a disproportionate amount of time dealing with problem employees. These general principles apply to all types of problem employees although how you apply them will depend on what is motivating the specific behavior that you consider to be a problem.

The first type of difficult employee is the "Gamer." Gamers see life as a competition and everyone as a competitor to be beaten. Gamers are not always seen as problems. Often, they can be quite successful. Only when these qualities are carried to extremes do Gamers become problematic, when a person's U Perspective focuses more on the act of winning than on what they win.

Gamers typically define situations in limiting terms and view every interaction as a zero sum game. They see limited resources and limited opportunities. They believe there can be only one real winner in any given situation. As a result, they believe that everything anyone else gets in some way comes at their expense. Because that is how they see the world, they may feel that it is okay to be manipulative or even deceitful. Gamers assume that the people they are dealing with do the same thing, or would if they had the opportunity, and that justifies their behavior.

The way to manage Gamers is to channel their competitive instincts productively. One way to do that is to portray the situations you are trying to manage as contests where you and the Gamer are on the same team competing against others - other companies, other divisions, etc.   Alternatively, allow Gamers to feel like they have won in their dealings with you by using the anchoring technique of initially seeking more than you actually expect to get from them and conceding reluctantly. The key to managing Gamers is to define situations in ways that allow them to consider themselves winners if they achieve the results you desire.

When managing Gamers set measurable goals against which results can be judged. You can also use the possibility of negative consequences, which will be seen as a loss, to prevent unacceptable behavior. Typically, Gamers apply a different standard to people they consider to be on their team, so spending the time necessary to develop a relationship with them may be helpful. Unfortunately, you cannot truly trust most Gamers even if you are working collaboratively with them. Therefore, when dealing with a Gamer document what you expect, what is agreed to and what is said. Fortunately we live in a world where e-mail allows us to document our conversations without seeming to be doing so.

Another difficult employee is the "Inflexible." Inflexibles are individuals who are rigid and resist change. They feel most comfortable in an orderly environment where procedures are clearly spelled out and responsibilities well defined. They like detailed rules, tend to be sticklers for complying with agreements and are uncomfortable with change. Where changing economic conditions and technology require frequent rapid adjustments, Inflexibles can impede your ability to implement necessary changes. On the other hand, Inflexibles often are hardworking and dedicated employees. In point of fact, that is usually the reason they resist change.

Fear is often what motivates their behavior. Inflexibles have succeeded because they understood what was expected of them. They have mastered the skills needed for those tasks, worked hard and done exactly what they were instructed to do. Inflexibles are afraid of change because they worry that they may not be as successful once the rules change. One of the hallmarks of Inflexibles is that they are risk averse. They also typically are highly motivated and want to do a good job. Inflexibles, however, believe that to do a good job they need to be in control. Change threatens that sense of control.

Understanding how to deal with Inflexibles requires understanding that U Perspective. To manage Inflexibles effectively you need to make them feel comfortable with anticipated changes and demonstrate how those changes will help them to be successful. Inflexibles respond well to expressions of confidence coupled with training. Training is important to reassure Inflexibles that they are in control of their own destiny.

When dealing with Inflexibles try to assign tasks and responsibilities that suit their temperament. Because of their U Perspective, Inflexibles usually do better in jobs that are more routine and regular. Also when dealing with Inflexibles, be careful what you say or write because they tend to be very literal. Make it clear that resistance to change is not an option. If an Inflexible continues to resist change, use counseling and coaching to spell out the consequences of their behavior at the same time that you offer support and training.

Another category of difficult employee is the "Avoider." Avoiders are procrastinators who hope that if they simply ignore a problem long enough it will go away. Avoiders can cause serious problems for an employer. Not only does the Avoider's work not get done, but others who depend on them are prevented from getting their work done. This can cause resentment among co-workers who, in order to get their own work done in a timely fashion, either have to do the Avoider's work themselves or spend an undue amount of time following up to get the Avoider to complete his or her tasks.

Avoiders need to be distinguished from the disorganized employees who cannot get work done efficiently due to problems with time management. Disorganized employees can be dealt with by providing training and appropriate time management tools such as planners. No amount of training will solve your problems with an Avoider. Dealing with Avoiders calls for a totally different response because they are coming from a very different U Perspective. Avoiders procrastinate not because they are lazy or inefficient but rather because they are risk averse. In fact, from their perspective when they don't deal with problems, they do go away. Other people do the work.

Not having to do the work, though, is usually not what motivates Avoiders; rather they are seeking to avoid responsibility. If they don't do the work, they cannot be held accountable if something goes wrong. By delaying, they often cause other people to step in and make decisions without their input allowing them to avoid responsibility if things don't go as planned. Avoiders portray themselves as thoughtful and analytical; sometimes they refer to themselves as perfectionists. They avoid making decisions by constantly seeking more information, shifting responsibility for any delay to the people that they are asking to provide information. That way if they are forced to make a decision and things don't work out well, they have someone else to blame because they had to make the decision without the benefit of the requested information.

In light of their U Perspective, the best way to deal with Avoiders is to make it riskier for them to delay, or not make a decision, than it would be for them to do something. Be very specific as to what you expect from an Avoider. Set precise timelines, place accountability clearly on them for accomplishing the expected work, don't allow for excuses and clearly set forth the consequences to the Avoider if the work does not get done on time. Do not allow Avoiders to pass off responsibility to others.

It also helps if you create an environment that supports, and encourages, reasonable risk taking. Managers promote Avoider behavior by focusing solely on successful outcomes. Intelligent risk taking - properly weighing potential risk against likely reward - still means that some decisions will not work out. If you positively reinforce individuals who take intelligent risks even when they don't turn out as hoped, you remove the primary reason for the Avoider's behavior - the fear that doing something will have negative consequences for them.

Another problem employee is the "Pleaser." There are two basic types of Pleasers: Socializers and Yes People. Pleasers are employees whose U Perspective centers on being liked. They seek to gain favor by pleasing others. Whether one is a Socializer or a Yes Person depends on whether one's efforts to be liked are primarily directed at peers (Socializers) or at the boss (Yes People).

There is nothing wrong with being friendly. However, it becomes a problem when an employee's primary focus is on being liked rather than on the work being produced. Socializers are often likeable, and you may, in actual fact, like them as individuals. Because they are likeable, Socializers often take advantage of their relationships to get others to do their work or to cover up for them. Moreover, they are adept socially and can usually provide reasons why work is not getting done. Socializers not only fail to do what they are expected to do, but they distract others from getting their work done as well.

When an employee's efforts at being liked are directed toward their boss, a similar problem exists. However, their boss may not consider the Socializer's behavior to be a problem or may even encourage their behavior. In many instances Yes People are manipulative and seek to gain favor by stroking their boss' ego. Do not reward Yes People behavior. That will only encourage more of the same and will create resentment among your other employees. Yes People may be motivated by lack of confidence or a desire to find an easy way to get ahead. If the motivation is the former then try to help build their confidence. If the latter, do not let them get away with the behavior.

When dealing with a Pleaser, whether a Socializer or a Yes Person, set clear and measurable goals against which to judge their work. Focus on the actual work being done and insist that Pleasers perform all the responsibilities that come along with their job. Spell out specific consequences for failing to meet those expectations. Do not let the fact that you like a Pleaser affect your follow through in imposing consequences if they fail to perform as requested.

Another common type of difficult employee is the "Intimidator." Intimidators are bullies and "know it alls" who get what they want by demanding and threatening. Typically Intimidators will behave differently with superiors than they do with their peers and subordinates. Intimidators gain support by being loud, persistent and implying that there will be consequences if you don't do what they want. Often with superiors they are overly agreeable, trying to give the impression that if you disagree with them you are also disagreeing with the boss. Intimidators try to dominate meetings and usually feel free to lose their temper.

If you have to deal with a peer who is an Intimidator don't take it personally. Force yourself to stay calm and remain in control. Take a break if necessary. Getting angry will only escalate the situation. As a matter of fact, sometimes speaking softly, but firmly, in response to an Intimidator can have a powerful inhibiting effect on that type of behavior. Intimidation only works if you let it. You can ignore attempts to intimidate or simply refuse to continue a discussion if a colleague is trying to get their way through intimidation. Insist on focusing on the issues. Humor can also be effective in changing the dynamics of your interactions with an Intimidator. It is hard to be intimidating to someone who has just made you smile. In the long run one way to prevent intimidation is to develop a friendly, professional relationship with the Intimidator. It is difficult to behave in an intimidating manner with someone that you consider a friend. If one of your subordinates is behaving this way with your other employees, your presence at critical meetings will deter them. So will openly encouraging a free exchange of ideas among your subordinates by the way you run your department. Since intimidating behavior often results from a lack of self confidence masked by public displays of arrogance, coaching Intimidators to develop skills that allow them to successfully engage people in more productive ways may also help.

Management is about motivating people. When you understand the U Perspective of your employees, you will understand how to get the best out of them. Even difficult employees can be successfully managed if you harness their U Perspective in constructive ways.

Chapter 13

The key to successful leadership today is influence, not authority.

Ken Blanchard

Leadership And The U Perspective

A new CEO is brought in to turn around a failing company. Once at the forefront of its industry, the company had recently fallen on hard times. For too many years executives received large bonuses by wringing profits out of their existing products and squelching innovations that might siphon market share away from those products. A culture of risk avoidance had developed, while an entrenched bureaucracy inhibited change.

The new CEO has a small window of opportunity to make dramatic changes and regain investor confidence. Fortunately, several promising products under development have survived despite a lack of nurturing by the prior leadership and these could rapidly be brought to market. While these new products are gaining ground the CEO needs to maintain the revenue stream from existing products. The CEO has identified one especially promising technology with the potential to help turn the company's fortunes around but anticipates resistance from those who have a vested stake in the existing product line. How does the CEO change the culture and gain the necessary support to successfully launch this new product?

This is not a task for a manager; it is the job of a leader. Many people have sought to understand what leadership is and how to achieve it. Much has been written on the topic and leadership has often been treated as if it were the holy grail of organizational success. Unfortunately, most efforts to distinguish leadership from management denigrate management skills. Though different, both are important to successful organizations. The relative importance of these skills varies depending on the needs of an organization at a given point in time. But, unless both types of skills are present, sooner or later an organization will flounder.

The concept of the U Perspective helps explain the difference between leadership and management skill sets and can be used to enhance both. Leadership is best understood as influencing others on a broader scale than simply managing them. Understood that way, the 3 Cs Influencing Method that we apply to influencing individuals in the context of managing, as well as when negotiating, selling and providing customer service, can also be applied to change the behavior of groups of individuals. This is the essence of leadership.

To lead you need to provide a different vision of how things should be done and to Convince others to take action that supports that vision; you need to Collaborate with people to find ways to satisfy their interests while furthering that vision; and you need to Create different structures to institutionalize that vision and build it into an organization's culture. But first you need to change behavior. As people incorporate the experiences resulting from that changed behavior into their U Perspective the organization's culture changes as well, institutionalizing the vision, fostering shared goals and values and transforming the organization.

Failure of a leader to align everyone's U Perspective with her own vision will inevitably result in people engaging in counterproductive behavior. Barbara was once asked to help a start-up work through the difficulties most organizations face when they land their first big customer. This client was an e-learning company that provided science curricula to secondary schools. They had a great product, good connections within the educational community and appeared to have priced their product properly. Yet they weren't able to get any school districts to agree to use their product.

After spending time with the CEO, Barbara was even more confused. He was extremely knowledgeable, was able to describe the product in non-technical language and, as a former teacher, he should have been able to speak to the U Perspective of his prospective customers. Barbara was baffled as to why not a single client had signed on until she went on a sales call with one of the company's salespeople. The problem was that the vision the CEO had created for the company and the resulting way his employees viewed their product ran directly counter to the U

Perspective of the school district administrators who would be deciding whether or not to buy the product.

The sales pitch employees used said it all:

> Some science teachers are really terrific and make the subject come alive for their class. Unfortunately, they are in the minority. Most science teachers are not able to impart their knowledge in a way that gets their students excited about the subject matter and many are primarily physical education instructors that aren't even that knowledgeable about the subject they are teaching. The science teachers that created our e-learning curricula are the best in the world and the resulting product is better than anything the district can expect from its own science teachers.

That, according to the CEO, was why school districts needed to purchase the product.

While this sales pitch may have been an accurate description of the way science was being taught in some school districts, suggesting to a school administrator that their science teachers were not that good and questioning their assignment practices challenged their U Perspective. This approach was unlikely to convince the target audience to buy the product.

Had the CEO created his vision for the company with the U Perspective of the customers in mind he would have emphasized the opportunities that e-learning offered for the best students, or that it allowed teachers to cover more ground, or to free up more time to help slower students. Focusing on how the e-learning product could be used to supplement what was being covered in class in a way that made the classroom day better for both the teachers and the students would have garnered more support from the science teachers who were ultimately his customers than belittling their teaching ability. Talking about how their product could be used to improve student test scores would have resonated with the U Perspective of the district administrators better than questioning their administrative decisions.

Leadership requires creating a vision that will appeal not only to the U Perspective of your employees but that of your customers as well.   Getting your employees to embrace the wrong vision can be as disastrous as not being able to get them to embrace your vision in the first place.

Barbara asked the CEO how he had come up with the corporate vision that his employees were using to try to sell their products. He explained that he had developed it when he was launching the company; it had worked very well with his investors. The investors obviously shared his U Perspective. Now, however, he had to sell his product and his employee needed to address the U Perspective of prospective customers. The CEO refused to recognize that the U Perspective of his customers differed from his own and that of his investors. As a result, the start-up never made a single sale. The product was a good one but the company failed because of poor leadership. The CEO insisted on trying to persuade others to see the world the way he did rather than accept and take advantage of the fact that from their point of view the world looked very different.

The 3 Cs Influencing Method provides the tools needed

to lead. Each approach, Convince, Collaborate and Create, harnesses the power of the U Perspective in a different way. Used together they enable a leader to gain the cooperation and support needed not only to execute his or her vision but also to build a corporate culture around that vision.

Recently, during breakfast at a conference where I was one of the speakers, I struck up a conversation with the woman sitting next to me, a marketing director at Novartis Pharmaceutical Corporation. During that discussion she described her CEO, Alex Gorsky, by saying that he had a way of "getting people to do whatever it took to get the job done." She added "you just don't want to let him down." That is the essence of leadership - the ability to motivate not just one individual but a whole organization to work together to advance a shared vision. That requires not only setting the direction of the organization but inspiring people who have very different U Perspectives to come together to support your vision.

When I heard Alex speak later that morning I understood why the marketing director felt the way that she did. Alex summed up what it takes to be a leader. "Leadership is about people," he said. "There is no way you can control every person in the organization yourself so you need to lead through others." Although he didn't use those words he clearly knows how to harness the power of the U Perspective to get the best out of all the people who work for him. "Leaders," he said, "understand the skills and talents of the individuals on their team and what motivates them and can put together complimentary skill sets." He also recognized that to be effective as a leader you have to keep in mind the U Perspective of the people to whom you report as well. "Ask yourself, what does my next level of management need to be successful. This will serve as radar telling you where you need to lead. Your team will appreciate it because it will make you more effective as a leader."

Too often leaders think that all they have to do is develop the right strategy, focus on the right products, determine how best to market them, structure an organization properly and everything else will fall into place. While developing sound strategies is important, as is structuring your organization properly, that is not enough to ensure success. Companies pay consultants lots of money to advise them on how to do those things. Often even after those consultants have recommended brilliant strategies, nothing happens. Why? Because simply articulating even the most brilliant strategy does not change the behavior of the people who have to implement it.

A leader needs not only to develop a vision that effectively meets changing conditions but go beyond that to motivate people to carry it out. Telling people what you want them to do is not sufficient. They have to want to do it. Otherwise any changes will, at best, be temporary. Leadership is needed to inspire everyone in the organization to work together to execute the same strategy. It requires using their U perspective to get people to do things differently and to embrace a common vision. All of their actions will then be guided by that vision. That vision will become part of the DNA of the organization. Changes in behavior come first. The experiences resulting from those changes in behavior will eventually impact people's values as they are incorporated into their U Perspective. In that way you can first change an organization's direction and then its culture.

Throughout this book I have talked about how individuals have different U Perspectives - how they are motivated by different things. Even the same individual will have more than one motivator that will come into play at different times and in different situations. How then can one use the U Perspective to lead an organization? That is exactly where leadership differs from management. In small organizations leaders may be able to know everyone and can try to motivate each employee individually. They can praise those motivated by recognition; have individualized compensation arrangements designed to motivate each individual to meet changing goals; and assign job tasks in ways that make the best use of each employee's skills and interests.

As organizations grow, however, leaders cannot know everyone personally nor can they motivate them directly, one by one, taking into account each person's unique U Perspective. Particularly as organizations increase in size, leaders need to build an organizational culture where everything that is done helps move the organization in the direction the leader seeks to take it. That way everyone in the organization will find something that motivates them to embrace the corporate vision and will behave accordingly, no matter what their job or what their U Perspective.

All systems in an organization must be designed to support and reinforce the culture and goals envisioned by its leaders. It is important that leaders communicate their vision consistently and regularly. Today's communications technology allows leaders to speak directly to everyone in an organization without ever actually meeting them. Organizations need to recruit people whose U Perspective is in sync with the direction they want to take the organization. Training and discipline need to be administered in ways that teach and encourage the behaviors needed to support that vision.

Sometimes a leader can inspire people by what they say. Others will be motivated by money; compensation systems need to reinforce the organizational culture, what is being said, and the business strategy being pursued. Above all, to take advantage of the U Perspectives to get the best out of those they seek to lead, leaders need to promulgate their vision in such a way that that everyone sees in it something that makes them want to support it. How can one do that if individuals have very different U Perspectives?

Great leadership not only allows for many points of view and many motivational triggers, it embraces them. Nowhere is this more apparent than during organizational mergers where, not only does a leader have to deal with different U Perspectives within each organization but also often has to contend with the clashing values of the cultures of very different organizations.

During the banking merger mania of the 1990s, banks were being bought out faster than you could use up your existing supply of checks. While this provided a boom for organizational consultants, it placed enormous strain on the people that worked at the banks. No sooner had they found out that they had survived the job cuts that followed a merger and made the necessary adjustments to new bosses, new systems and new procedures, than the cycle would start all over again. While the shareholders did well, employees ended up battered and shell-shocked.

Barbara had the opportunity during this time period to work with the human resources department of one of the mega banks that was being formed as a result of the merger of seven smaller banks. Her role was to help them create a vision statement and then design an organizational structure that would deliver on that vision. To achieve a combined vision for the seven banks represented in the new organization, one where everyone would feel appreciated and valued, was a daunting task. Fortunately, the Senior Vice President of Human Resources responsible for managing the merger was a true leader. She understood the power of the U Perspective.

People's U Perspectives, and therefore their expectations, are based on their past experiences and the different organizational cultures from which they come. Organizational culture is based in part on what is referred to as legacy. Legacy speaks about the contributions that employees have made towards past goals. In other words, legacy celebrates people - the same people who are going to do the work in the new organization. By recognizing and honoring people who exemplify the values and behaviors that a leader is seeking to inspire, others are encouraged to emulate them. Because each of these seven organizations had very different legacies, creating a vision that everyone would buy into was extremely difficult. Adding to that difficulty was the fact that each of these seven organizations had gone out of their way to try to differentiate themselves from each other as a way to attract customers. Now, employees were being asked to come up with a single unified vision while working with people they had previously considered to be their competition – the enemy.

At first this task seemed nearly impossible. However, by recognizing the power of the U Perspective, they were able to create a vision that everyone embraced. Instead of drafting a written values statement that set forth the new vision for the combined entity, they developed an image. An artist was brought in to listen to the group as thay talked through all the issues that the new organization would face as it reorganized itself. The attendees were asked to talk about what had made each of the former organizations great and how the new organization could incorporate what was best about each of the pre-existing organizations. By the end of the meeting the artist had prepared a 6 foot by 10 foot drawing that incorporated key success stories from each of the predecessor organizations that everyone agreed encompassed the values that they wanted the new organization to embrace. The resulting picture told the story of seven successful organizations moving through their individual histories into an even better future where everyone would be valued for what they brought to the merged company.

By using icons from the past as a foundation for the new vision, everyone was able to leave the meeting with a strong understanding of, and commitment to, the new vision. Moreover, in that vision everyone could see something that was important to them - something that reinforced their U Perspective. To promote that vision and motivate employees throughout the organization the drawing was printed on tee shirts and mouse pads which were then distributed throughout the entire company. The merger proceeded smoothly and the initial goals that had been set for the combined entity were quickly reached. That merger is still considered by people in the industry to be one of the most successful of the period.

The Convince, Create and Collaborate tools that allow you to influence people one-to-one also can be used to change organizational behavior. How do you apply the 3 Cs Influencing Method to lead an organization, a department or a team? Let's start with Convince. Behavior is informed by how people see things and what they care about. The U Perspective, when used as a leadership tool, is not about trying to change people's values to mirror your own. It is about informing and motivating behavior that is consistent not only with their values but also the culture of the organization you are seeking to build. Simply sharing your vision of the future, no matter how powerful the presentation, will not automatically persuade people to change their behavior in ways necessary to further that vision unless they believe that where you are taking the organization is consistent with their U Perspective. People do not change their behavior simply because change is needed. Most people are comfortable with what they know even though it may not be working especially well. While they may acknowledge that some change is essential, people tend to resist change out of fear that any particular change may make matters worse for them.

To get people to embrace your vision and change their

behavior, you have to appeal to their U Perspective. Sometimes that means giving those you are seeking to persuade something tangible that they value. That is why compensation drives behavior. For certain individuals money is the primary motivator. We generally want our salespeople to be motivated by money. That is why most companies pay their sales force some form of commission or incentive bonus. Alternatively, you may first need to Convince people to change their behavior by demonstrating that there will be negative consequences for them if they continue doing things the way they have done them in the past.

While essential, changes to compensation structures are not usually enough by themselves to propel change throughout an organization. The U Perspective concept explains why. Most people are not motivated solely by money; neither do most organizations have sufficient resources available to use compensation as the sole motivator for change. Even salespeople need recognition for a job well done from time to time to keep them motivated. Because money is a part in most people's U Perspective, however, without the proper compensation structure to support other motivators, change will elude an organization. Moreover, the way you compensate someone sends a message to them about what an organization cares about. If you preach the importance of customer service but pay people based on the number of transactions they handle, they soon get the message that speed is more important than the quality of the service they provide.

The impact of a poorly designed compensation structure is a testament to the power of compensation to either reinforce a leader's vision or to undermine it. In the face of a bankruptcy one company sought to change behavior by changing their compensation structure. The vision the corporation's CEO espoused was a balanced one seeking to increase sales and profits by offering quality merchandise at prices that provided a good value to customers. To support that strategy he decided to redesign the compensation system. To increase market share, he provided bonuses to the people who could directly impact sales -- buyers, salespeople and marketers -- based solely on increases in total sales. To be able to sell merchandise at lower prices, he provided bonuses to those individual's who were responsible for operating the business - operations managers, IT, accounting, etc. - based solely on their ability to reduce costs. What he got was increased sales and reduced cost in the short run at the expense of poor customer service and a reduced profit margin in the long run. Since the bonuses of those individuals who could impact sales were based on gross revenues, sales were achieved at the expense of eroding profit margin. Since the bonuses of those individual's who could most directly affect costs did not measure the impact achieving those savings had on sales and customer service they often were attained at the expense of poorer customer service and lower profit margins in the long run.

Convince centers on enhancing the perceived value of what you are proposing. For a leader that is your vision. To change an organization's culture first you need to get people to engage in different behaviors, those that support your vision. The stronger an organization's existing culture (the employee's shared way of doing and thinking about things) the more difficult it is to get people to see things except in terms of what has previously existed, resulting in the failure of most efforts to implement a new organizational vision. That is both the power of "culture" as well as its fatal flaw. It guides behavior but also inhibits change.

Convince uses anchoring, legitimacy, active listening, purposeful questioning and how you deliver your message to encourage behavior that advances your vision, eventually leading to a change in organizational culture. That is where the U Perspective comes into play. The key to convincing someone is listening to them. That is equally true in organizations. Good leaders ask lots of questions and listen to the responses. They spend time listening to those they seek to lead. If you listen people will tell you what they need to hear in order to be persuaded to change their behavior. Understanding the motivators that drive an organizational culture will enable you to change that culture or harness it to support your vision.

People often think that they aren't being heard. We all have a need to be heard. At the heart of any relationship, whether professional or personal, is a belief that the other person cares about what you have to say. For a leader to be effective, those he or she seeks to lead need to believe that the leader cares about them and is acting in their best interests. Making sure people feel that you have heard them is the first step toward gaining their support and cooperation. In order for someone to be open to listening to you, they have to feel that you are listening to them. Leadership always begins with listening.

Leaders not only need to listen, but they also need to care about what people say. People can usually tell if someone is not being sincere. True leaders genuinely care about the people they lead. General Norman Schwarzkopf tells a story about Collin Powell and Ronald Reagan that brings this point home. Collin Powell had suggested a course of action to President Reagan. The President had initially disagreed with Powell but eventually was persuaded to go along with his suggestion. As things would have it the strategy was not successful; in fact, it was a dismal failure. At a press conference President Reagan was asked, "Who came up with such an ill-conceived strategy?" With Collin Powell standing in the back of the room, President Reagan responded, "I did." According to General Norman Schwarzkopf, Powell later told the General that at that moment a tear came to his eye and he thought to himself, I'd follow that person anywhere. That is true leadership.

Leaders also need to build teams. Getting the different parts of an organization to work together in furtherance of a common vision is essential. That is where Collaborate comes into play. Working with the executive team requires identifying different interests and finding ways to satisfy those interests. It requires understanding people's U Perspectives and putting together teams where the members' skills and motivators complement one another. All the Collaborate tools are needed to enable a leader to get teams to work together in furtherance of the organizational vision.

Finally, a momentary change in behavior is not enough. The changes that support a new vision need to become part of a new culture. Those changes need to be institutionalized. That is where the Create techniques play a role. Create requires looking at the organizational structure differently. It calls for bringing in different people, eliminating others and changing the way people interact. Organizational structure can support or inhibit the changes one is seeking to make. Employing Create techniques that reinforce the changes you are seeking to implement will enable you to build an enduring culture that supports a new vision.

In the end, harnessing the power of the U Perspective will enable you to get what you want whether dealing with an individual or leading an organization. Accepting and leveraging, rather than trying to change, people's values and the way they see the world is the key to gaining their cooperation and changing their behaviors. Do not assume that others share your values, see a situation the same way you do, or care about what you care about. Allow them to support your vision because it supports their values and what they care about. Harness people's U Perspectives to motivate, to gain their support and to change their behavior. Ultimately changing someone's behavior will impact their U Perspective. In that way leaders can change an organization's culture in a way that furthers their vision and continues to do so long after they are gone. That is why successful leaders instinctively understand and use the U Perspective.

Index

Other Books by Lee E. Miller

A Woman's Guide to Successful Negotiations – How to Convince Collaborate and Create Your Way to Agreement

Employment Discrimination

Get More Money on Your Next Job

Extended Workshops, Materials, and Interactive CDs created with Barbara Jackson

NegotiationPlus 101: The Art of Getting What You Want

CustomerServicePlus: High Performance Customer Service

SalesPlus: The Art of Selling

Managing Difficult Employees

InterviewingPlus: Hiring the Best

InterviewingPlus: Getting the Job

Active Listening: The Art of Listening

ABOUT THE AUTHORS

LEE E. MILLER, a graduate of Harvard Law School, is the Managing Director of NegotiationPlus.com and the co-host of the Your Career Doctors Radio Show. An Adjunct Professor of Management at Seton Hall University, he is the 2003 and 2005 recipient of the Business School's Award for Teaching Excellence. Lee is the co-author, with his daughter, of *A Woman's Guide to Successful Negotiating* (McGraw Hill) a featured book on Good Morning America and The Early Show and selected by Atlanta Woman magazine as one of the 50 best books for professional women. He is also the author the best selling *Get More Money on Your Next Job* (McGraw Hill). He has written a monthly career column for Monster.com and is a contributor to the Wall Street Journal Online. Previously he was the Senior Vice President of Human Resources at TV Guide Magazine, USA Networks and Barney's New York Inc., a Vice President of Labor and Employee Relations at R.H. Macy & Co. Inc. and a partner and co-chair of the employment and labor group of one of the largest law firms in New Jersey. Lee is the former Chair of the International Association of Corporate and Professional Recruiters and Secretary to the Union County Motion Picture Advisory Board.

BARBARA JACKSON is the President of Mayberry Consulting and the co-host of the Your Career Doctors Radio Show. A graduate of Providence College with a Masters in Public Administration from the Maxwell School of Government at Syracuse University, she served as the Budget Director for the Commonwealth of Massachusetts. She has also served as the Commissioner of Surface Transit at the Department of Transportation for the City of New York; First Deputy Commissioner of the NYC Department of Ports and Trade , VP Finance and Budget for NJ Transit and Deputy Director in NYC's Office of Management and Budget. Barbara is a pioneer in the field of distance learning, working with several of MIT's Distance Learning Center's offshoots and other web-based learning startups and is a successful entrepreneur who has started and sold several companies.

UP: Influence Power and the U Perspective
The Art of Getting What You Want

ORDERING: To order additional copies of this book, send a check or money order, or provide your credit card information. Copies are $18.95 USD per book plus $3.95 for shipping and handling.

Send this form with your payment to:

Career Doctors Inc., 45 Park Avenue, Suite # 240, Morristown, NJ 07960

To order by credit card: ☐ MC ☐ Visa

Card # _____ *Exp. Date* _____

For information about bulk orders or foreign delivery contact Your Career Doctors Press at ahrgrp@earthlink.net For email orders send credit card and mailing information to ahrgrp@ earthlink.net or order on line at YourCareerDoctors.com

ADDITIONAL INFORMATION: If you would like to know more about the authors and their availability for training at your organization go to the YourCareerDoctors.com website or contact Your Career Doctors Press at ahrgrp@earthlink.net. If you'd like the authors to hold a book signing at a bookstore in your area have the bookstore contact us.

For more information on other Your Career Doctors products and services send this form to the address above: ☐ Other Books ☐ Interactive Training CDs ☐ Online Training ☐ Speaking ☐ Workshops ☐ Organizational Training or Consulting ☐ One on One Coaching ☐ Other products.

Name _____

Address_____

_____

City_____ State_____ Zip_____

E-mail Address _____